MUSCLECAR
COLOR • HISTORY

CHEVROLET
SS

ROBERT GENAT

MBI Publishing Company

Dedication

To Sharon Stein, a *Super* human being and one hell of a good *Sport.*

First published in 2000 by MBI Publishing Company, 729 Prospect Avenue, PO Box 1, Osceola, WI 54020-0001 USA

© Robert Genat, 2000

MBI Publishing Company books are also available at discounts in bulk quantity for industrial or sales-promotional use. For details write to Special Sales Manager at Motorbooks International Wholesalers & Distributors, 729 Prospect Avenue, PO Box 1, Osceola, WI 54020-0001 USA.

Library of Congress Cataloging-in-Publication Data
Genat, Robert.
    Chevrolet SS / Robert Genat.
        p. cm. — (Musclecar color history)
    Includes index.
    ISBN 0-7603-0715-6 (pbk. : alk. paper)
      1. Chevrolet automobile—History. 2. Muscle cars—History. I. Title. II. MBI Publishing Company muscle car color history.
    TL215.C5 G23 2000
    629.222'0973—dc21   99-056531

On the front cover: Chevy was at the top of its horsepower and musclecar image game when the 1970 SS454 Chevelle was introduced. At that time, the streets were a sniper's nest filled with high-horsepower competition ready to pick off any unwary intruder. The 1970 SS454 Chevelle proved to be asphalt assault vehicle capable of humiliating the toughest competitor. There was nothing to suggest that the 1970 SS454 Chevelle was an ordinary transportation car—it was a steroid-intensified musclecar that sweated testosterone from every pore.

On the frontispiece: Every 1967 Super Sport Camaro had SS emblems on the front fenders, gas filler cap, and in the center of the grille. Those equipped with the 350 cubic inch engine had special grille and gas cap emblems that displayed SS350.

On the title page: In the early 1960s, Chevrolet found a way to bottle lightening—they called it the Impala Super Sport. The 1964 Impala SS was the most refined Super Sport to date offering an exceptional level of performance an unmistakable style at an affordable price.

On the back cover: Main image: In 1969, Chevy added a new pair of chrome hood vents to the Super Sport Camaro, each having four simulated stacks. The combination of RS and SS options had proved successful and was again available on the 1969 models. The revised front end required new headlight doors for the hidden headlights with the RS option. Three attractive horizontal windows were added to each door. All SS model Camaros had blacked out grilles, except for the cars that were painted black. *Inset image:* The new federally mandated 5-mile per hour bumper took precedence and its mass almost overwhelmed the front end. SS models in 1973 had a blacked out grille with an SS emblem in the center and dual sport mirrors.

Edited by Sara Perfetti
Designed by Laura Henricksen
Printed in Hong Kong

Contents

Acknowledgments

Thanks to the following Super Sport owners for taking the time to let me photograph their cars: Stuart Glass, Gary Clark, Steve and Debbie Spirkoff, Bud Miller, Casey Patelski, Mike Adamson, Glen Konkle, Bob Keck, Robb Newman, Jim Ross, Joe and Sandy Shea, Greg Lambert, Steve Minard, Dale Armstrong, Tom Duncan, Roy Hernandez, Steve Halluska, Pete Stadtfield, Mike Reiaha, Bob Inhoff, Leroy and Judy Williams, Carl and Jilleen Strobel, Tim Stout, and Steve Doro. Great cars, great folks!

Thanks to Julia Daniel at General Motors Media Archives for the beautiful Chevrolet archival photography and to Dan Hubbert, Nancy Libby, and Carolyn Landrum at Chevrolet for all their help. Thanks to NHRA for the use of its photos, and the Late Great Chevy organization. A special thanks to Chuck Jordan, Dave Holls, Ron Hill, Blaine Jenkins, and Dick Keinath for their diligent work on these cars while at GM and for sharing their experiences with me. Good work, guys!

Thanks to the following motorheads for their varied contributions to this project: Joe McCaron, Jeff Glass, Jim Glass, Dan Burger, Joe Veraldi, and Dean Westmorland. And a special thanks to the following photographers for the use of their excellent SS images: Mike Mueller, Dale Amy, Jim Knight, and Chris Richardson.

Introduction

Car guys are a breed of their own. We can vividly remember the type of mag wheels that were on a car we raced against in 1966, but the date of our wedding anniversary remains a mystery. Specific car images play in our minds like a slide show. As Super Sport images dance through my head, I can clearly remember the first SS Chevy I ever saw. It was a red-on-red 1962 409-powered sport coupe. The first SS I ever drove belonged to a girl I dated—Honduras Maroon, black interior, 283, Powerglide, power steering and brakes. Funny, I can't remember a thing about the girl.

My brother indoctrinated me to Chevys at an early age. Three of his cars that stand out in my mind are his 1963 409 Impala, 1966 SS396 Chevelle, and big block 1970 Monte Carlo. These cars left an indelible mark on my youthful automotive psyche. There has always been a mystique surrounding Chevy's Super Sport special trim and high-performance engines. The brawny appeal of a big block SS Camaro or SS454 Chevelle easily dispels any biases a Ford or Mopar lover may have. The SS emblem on the side of a Chevy gave notice to the world that this car had the right stuff. In most instances, Chevrolet offered a solid combination of performance engine and chassis hardware to go with those daunting SS emblems.

One of the most interesting parts of the SS story is the enthusiasm shared by the people who designed and built these cars. Looking back, it was a wonderful time to be in the automotive business. Money was plentiful and there were very few restrictions to limit their creativity. Some of the brightest visionaries in automotive history were at General Motors at that time. Men like Bill Mitchell, Bunkie Knudsen, Ed Cole, Irv Rybicki, Clare MacKichan, Henry Haga, Harry Barr, Vince Piggins, and Pete Estes were the ones who held the hammers and stoked the fires when the wonderful SS cars we cherish today were forged.

Chevy's Impala was completely restyled for the 1961 model year. It was the first full-size Chevy designed entirely under the watchful eye of Bill Mitchell, who followed Harley Earl as General Motors' vice president of styling. The 1961 Impala was also the first Chevy production car to be adorned with SS emblems and trim. One of the requirements of the SS option was the inclusion of one of several high-performance 348-ci engines or the new 409.

Chapter 1
Impala SS 1961–1964
Chevrolet's Jump Start to the Performance Era

The economy in America was good following World War II. The industrial machine that had turned out bombers, tanks, and aircraft carriers was quickly shifted to durable goods, and with only a few minor adjustments, America's economy continued to grow into the 1960s. Early in 1961, the country entered an economic adjustment period and sales of durable goods, including automobiles, were down. Toward the end of the year the trend quickly reversed, but overall, auto industry sales were down 15 percent. General Motors faired only slightly better with a 14-percent reduction in total sales compared to its 1960 levels. The only bright spot was the fourth-quarter sales figures, which were near record levels. In 1961, General Motors produced a total of 3.1 million cars and trucks, 1.6 million of which were Chevrolet passenger cars.

Spearheading General Motors sales in 1961 was the Chevy line-up, which included the Corvair and the all-new, full-size Biscayne, Bel Air, and Impala. These were the first Chevys designed under the guidance of Bill Mitchell, Harley Earl's successor as vice president of design at General Motors. The 1961 Chevy's rear wings were only imaginary, outlined by chrome across the rear deck. Headroom and overall vehicle height on the 1961 Chevrolet was increased by 2 inches—a response to criticism directed at the 1959 and 1960 Chevrolets for their low rooflines and minimal headroom. The overall length was 1.8 inches shorter than the 1960 Chevrolet. These changes represented a major shift from the design philosophy of Harley Earl, who liked his cars low and long.

The 1961 Chevrolet body was completely new. Under Bill Mitchell's direction, Clare MacKichan came up with the design for the bob-tail rear deck featuring six round taillights. Young Chevrolet designer Paul Deesen worked out the front end and was able to carry over the Chevrolet name in block letters on the hood. The new Impala body was a very conservative design compared to its predecessor. The raised roofline and resultant redesign of the A-pillar eliminated the wrap-around windshield used on 1958 through 1960 Chevrolets, which didn't bother owners whose knees had been bruised by the lower corner of the windshield's structure when entering or exiting the front seat. The 1961 Impala was available as a station wagon, four-door sedan, four-door hardtop, two-door sport coupe, convertible, or two-door sedan. The Impala two-door sedan was a one-time offering not previously available nor ever again produced.

Supporting the 1961 Chevrolet was the same X-frame design that was introduced in 1958. In 1959, the wheelbase had been stretched to 119 inches and the rear suspension geometry revised. For 1961, the frame's rear side-members were shortened, due to the reduced overhang. The short and long arm coil spring independent front suspension was basically the same as the one introduced in 1958. New for 1961 were roller-type front wheel bearings replacing the ball-type bearings. A 0.68-inch diameter front sway bar was standard equipment on all Impalas. The only major change to the 1961 Chevy's underbody was the relocation of the gas tank, which was moved from under the luggage compartment floor

Tail fins—so outrageous two years earlier—were now only imaginary on the 1961 Impala, traced by thin chrome moldings across the deck lid. In the center of the V on the deck lid, and adjacent to the Impala script on the quarter panel, are the SS emblems, inlayed in red.

to the area between the trunk and rear axle. This allowed the luggage compartment to have a very deep well, a big selling point against Ford's shallow trunk. The relocation of the gas tank required the addition of a gas filler door to the left quarter panel.

The interior of the 1961 Chevrolet was completely redesigned. The most dramatic change was the new instrument panel. The jet cockpit design of the 1960 instrument panel was replaced with a more upscale look. The 120-mile-per-hour speedometer was long, horizontal, and deeply recessed into a large cove. At the base of the steering column were three small circular bezels that housed the gas gauge, temperature gauge, and a clock, which was standard on the Impala and optional on all other models. The glove box was moved to the center of the instrument panel, easily accessible by

both driver and passenger. The optional AM radio was installed above the glove box. The standard manual tune radio stickered for an additional $53.80, and the deluxe, push-button radio added $62.45 to the price of the car. On the Impala hardtops and convertibles, the customer had the choice of a front or rear antenna.

Up until 1961, Chevrolet seat cushions and seat backs were flat, and resembled the bench-like seats in a bus. Due to cost, any additional detailing of General Motors' seats was reserved for the higher priced Pontiac, Buick, Oldsmobile, or Cadillac. One trick used to detail the seats on these upscale cars was to sew in a design pad (strips of foam under the upholstery) to give shape to the seat. In 1961, the seats of the Chevrolet Impala featured a design pad consisting of 3-inch-wide strips of 1/2-inch-thick foam. These seemingly insignificant strips gave the cushion contour and definition. The design, worked out by Chevrolet interior designer Blaine Jenkins, was approved by General Manager Ed Cole, who liked to put the money where it would be seen when the potential customer looked into the car at the dealer's showroom. The cost for the design pad was only $1.50 per Impala, a small price for the added refinement.

The Super Sport option was added late in the 1961 model year to boost the sporty image of the Impala. The 1961 Chevrolet Super Sport was a combination of exterior and interior trim items and a wealth of performance options—arguably creating the first super car. The Super Sport's unique specifications were documented in a February 1961 amendment to Chevrolet's 1961 passenger car engineering specifications, originally published in October 1960. The Super Sport option was created too late to make it into the regular Chevrolet sales brochure for new car introduction in the fall of 1960, so a special brochure featuring an illustration of a four-door Impala hardtop in Super Sport trim was printed and shipped to dealers. Chevrolet did not keep statistics on exactly how many customers selected the Super Sport option, but estimates show 450 were sold in 1961—doubtfully any four-doors.

Body trim for the 1961 Super Sport included special SS deck lid and quarter panel emblems with a red inlay. Added to the standard 1961 full wheel cover was a tri-bar simulated knock-off spinner. It was on the 1961 Super Sport that Chevrolet first used thin-line, white sidewall tires (8.00x14). These four-ply, rayon-belted, thin-line tires were not available on any other Chevrolet models in 1961—only the Super Sport. All Super Sport wheel rims were painted black, regardless of body color.

The Super Sport interior consisted of the standard Impala trim, plus a few extras. A passenger assist bar was added to the right side of the instrument panel, in part because of the large open area there. The bar, patterned after the passenger assist bars used on the Pontiac Bonneville, was designed by Chevrolet designer Corwin Hanson. He inserted an Impala SS logo into the left end and added three lines, called "go-fasters" by interior designers, to the grip. Behind the steering wheel, mounted in a chrome cup, was a Sun tachometer, like those used by the most prominent racers at that time. A Sun tach on the steering column of a car on the street was seen as a badge of courage. The Impala's tach was prominently visible at the 10 o'clock position on the steering column to allow full view of the speedometer, and swept from 0 to 7,000 rpm with no redline indicated. A small rectangular chrome console, designed by Chevrolet interior designer Blaine Jenkins, was added when a Super Sport was equipped with a four-speed manual transmission. Super Sports equipped with the optional Powerglide were column-shifted and did not have the special console.

A problem with the 1961 Super Sport option was the high cost of the mandatory options the customer had to order just to get the SS trim. The buyer was required to order one of three high-performance 348-ci engines or the 409. Transmission choices were limited to the four-speed manual or the high-performance Powerglide, which was available only with the 305-horsepower 348. Also required were heavy-duty front and rear springs and shocks, and thin-line white sidewall tires. Power-assisted steering and brakes had to be added to the list. Finally, a padded instrument panel and tachometer rounded out the list of "must haves." These required options pushed-up the sticker price of the Impala by more than $600 before the $50 SS option could even be added. Add a radio, heater, and a few other options and that new 1961 Impala

Chevrolet designers replaced the jet cockpit-style instrument panel of the 1960 Chevy with a new "dog house" design. Impala interiors were well appointed with cloth and vinyl seats. The Super Sport option added the passenger assist bar, small floor shifter console, and padded instrument panel. This 1961 SS also has factory air conditioning.

A Sun tachometer was an accessory always found on the hottest race cars of the era. Chevrolet offered this 7,000-rpm version as an option with any V-8 for $48.45. It was one of the required options when the Super Sport option was selected.

SS could sticker over $4,000—more than the base price of a new 1961 Corvette.

The SS option required that one of three high-performance 348-ci engines or the new 409 be selected from the option list. The 348, commonly known as the "W" engine, was introduced in 1958. In the mid-1950s, the Chevrolet engineering team of John Rausch, Howard Kehrl, and Donald McPherson was given the task of developing Chevrolet's next-generation V-8. Their goal was to design an engine that would adapt to a broad range of compression ratios, cubic-inch displacements, and horsepowers. The new engine would serve as a platform for current truck and passenger car accessories. Whatever this team developed had to fit within the same engine compartment as the small block. And, out of the box, the new engine had to be more powerful than the current V-8.

Chevrolet engineers began work on several designs for the new engine. Following the standard General Motors practice of assigning codes to experimental engines, Chevy engineers worked on two variants of the small block: "X" and "Y." The design that would eventually become the 348 was coded with the letter "W." (Popular urban legend incorrectly maintains that the "W" came from the scalloped design of the valve covers.) The "X" and "Y" small block variants were both of 300-cubic-inch displacement, but each engine design used different combinations of bore and stroke to attain its

displacement. Because of the casting technology of the mid-1950s, the Chevy design team felt that in order to increase the displacement of the small block to over 300 cubic inches, a new block design would be needed. The "W" engine was the alternative design. It fulfilled all of the original criteria and, because of its unique design, offered several other advantages.

According to Dick Keinath, former Chevrolet engine engineer who was a member of the "W" engine's design team, the "W" engine was initially developed in two displacements: 307 and 348. "The 307 never made it off the drawing board," says Keinath. "We had a lot of power coming out of the 283 and felt we'd better jump to 348."

The 348-ci "W" block was a compact design. It was only 1.5 inches longer and 2.6 inches wider than the small block. Amazingly, the 348's overall height was 0.8 inch lower than the small block, but it outweighed the small block by over 140 pounds. The new 348 "W" engine was designed with its chassis mounts on the side of the block. Also retained was the provision to be front-mounted like the 1955 through 1957 small blocks. Similar to the small block, the "W" block included a right-hand-mounted starter and fuel pump and rear-mounted distributor. These features, and a similar rear face of block, made the new "W" design compatible as an optional engine in the same chassis as a small block.

Chevrolet engineers felt that one of the keys to the small block's performance was its ratio of bore to

On the 1961 Super Sport, Chevrolet added a tri-bar spinner to the center of the Impala's full wheel cover. Narrow-band white wall tires were available only on the 1961 Super Sport Impala.

stroke. When designing the 348, they used a similar ratio. The ratio of bore to stroke in the 283 (3.87x3.00) was 0.77; and in the 348 (4.125x3.25) it was 0.78. The short length of the block and the short stroke of the engine combined to produce a very sturdy crankshaft, and offered other benefits. "We liked the lower piston speed, shorter connecting rod, and lower height of the complete engine," Keinath says.

The "W" block's compact overall design was due in part to the staggered layout of the intake and exhaust valves. The engineers felt that if they were to increase cubic inches (to almost 50 cubic inches per cylinder), the valve sizes had to be increased. If these larger valves were in a straight line, they would require more space (a longer block) than if they were staggered. The staggering of the valves was made easier by the stud-mounted stamped-steel rocker arm similar to the one used on the small block. This staggered valve arrangement also necessitated the "W" engine's uniquely scalloped valve covers. The new cylinder heads, which were wider and slightly longer than the small block's heads, accounted for a substantial part of the increased engine weight. These heads also lacked a traditional combustion chamber. Small recesses around the valves were the only indentations in an otherwise flat underside surface. The combustion chamber was contained within the block.

While the "W" engine was being designed, there were eight different head designs in production for the small block. Chevrolet engineers reasoned that a single head design for the "W" engine would be more economical to produce. To create the wedge-shaped combustion chamber in the block, a 74-degree cut was made across the cylinder bores instead of the traditional 90-degree slice. Placing the combustion chamber in the cylinder was not an original design. Mercedes-Benz had already pioneered the design in one of their engines of that era. With the combustion chamber in the block, changes in compression ratio could be made by simply replacing pistons. In addition to piston design, reliefs were cut into the upper portion of the cylinder wall to vary compression ratios. Instead of casting a new head with a revised chamber, Chevrolet had only to change a tool and it had a new combustion chamber. The theory of the design was excellent—an easily reconfigurable fully machined combustion chamber. Reality proved that there were some flaws in the design concept.

The combustion chamber in the block restricted the engineers from optimizing the shape of the chamber as they might have, had it been cast into the head. "I do believe," recalls Keinath, "that some

Chevy's only advertisement for the new Impala Super Sport was in the May 1961 issue of Hot Rod magazine. A large photo features a driver's-eye-view of the interior with ad copy touting the excitement of Chevy's high-performance engines.

of the volumetric efficiency was suffering from the high ratio of surface to volume of the combustion chamber." Keinath is referring to the surface area of the combustion chamber versus its volume. A perfect combustion chamber has low surface area in relation to its overall volume. A perfect chamber would be a sphere—maximum volume with minimum surface area (the hemi for instance). The 348's combustion chamber was in the block and could not be reduced to increase compression, except by the use of pistons with raised areas to fill up that volume. Those raised areas created more surface area within the combustion chamber—a less than ideal situation. "When we would increase compression ratio by putting a bump on one side of the piston, that would increase the surface area but reduce the volume—going backwards, as far as trying to come up with a lower surface area." This increased surface meant that the 348's combustion chamber burn ratio was lower than that in an engine like the small

Added to the 1961 Impala's instrument panel was a bright anodized aluminum overlay. This overlay extended from the light switch on the left to the radio, then downward, covering the center-mounted glove box. Added to the SS models were the column-mounted tach and the passenger assist bar on the right. *Copyright 1978–1999 GM Corp. Used with permission of GM Media Archives*

block. "We finally got it to come around pretty well," Keinath recalls. "It was a combination of things, a lot of porting and camshaft work—but we couldn't do much with the chambers."

The new 348 engine was available as an option in 1958. Rated at 250 horsepower, the base 348 was equipped with a single four-barrel carburetor. The same engine with three two-barrel carburetors was rated at 280 horsepower. In 1959 the top-rated 348 was increased to 315 horsepower and in 1960 to 335 horsepower. In 1961, there were five 348s available, with the top-rated engine at 350 horsepower. To add the Super Sport option to a 1961 Impala, the customer was required to add one of three high-performance 348-ci engines or the new 409.

The tamest 348 available for the 1961 Super Sport was the 305-horsepower version, named the "Special Turbo-Thrust." The 305's short block was identical to the 250- and 280-horsepower 348s, which included a hydraulic camshaft and cast 9.5:1 pistons. The extra horsepower was gained by new heads that had larger intake (2.07 diameter) and exhaust (1.72 diameter) valves and an aluminum intake manifold fitted with a Carter AFB carburetor. The 305-horsepower 348 was also the only engine available for the Super Sport that could be mated to the Powerglide transmission.

The 340-horsepower, 348-ci engine shared the Special Turbo-Thrust name with the 305 version. From the exterior it looked the same as the 305 with a single Carter AFB (500 cfm) on an aluminum intake. It also had the same large valve heads, but internally it was quite different. The pistons were forged with a compression ratio of 11.25:1. The 340's mechanical camshaft had a longer (287-degree) duration. In the Super Sport, the 340-horsepower engine could only be backed with a four-speed manual transmission.

At 350 horsepower, the Special Super Turbo-Thrust was the highest horsepower 348-ci engine ever offered. It was identical to the 340-horsepower version except the single four-barrel was replaced with three Rochester two-barrel carburetors. Three two-barrel carburetors, commonly called "tri-power," first appeared on a General Motors car in 1957 when Oldsmobile introduced its J2 system. Soon, every GM division except Buick was offering its version of tri-power. The center-mounted carburetor facilitated low-speed driveability and economy, and the end carburetors were there for power when needed.

Coinciding with the release of the Super Sport option was the announcement of the 409. Basically, the 409 was a bored and stroked 348. The bore was increased by 3/16 inch to 4.1325 inches; and the stroke was increased by 1/4 inch to 3.500 inches. Because the 348 block could not reliably be bored and the lower end had to be modified for the longer crank throws, a new block had to be cast to facilitate the new internal dimensions. Forged aluminum pistons were fitted to the 409 at an advertised compression ratio of 11.25.

The 1961 409 heads were the same as the 348 heads, with a few exceptions. They had slightly larger pushrod holes to accommodate the larger diameter (3/8 inch) pushrods. The valve spring bosses were enlarged to accept single springs with dampeners. And the 409's solid lifter camshaft had an intake duration of 317 degrees and an exhaust duration of 301.

All of these early 409s used a single four-barrel aluminum intake manifold which was, with one exception, the same one used on the 340-horsepower 348. The throttle bores were opened up on the primary side to accept the large (600 cfm) Carter AFB. A dual-point Delco distributor, with no vacuum advance, provided the spark. The exhaust manifolds were the same as the ones used on high-performance 348s with 2-1/2 inch openings to the mufflers.

The first two 409 engines were publicly seen at the 1961 NHRA Pomona Winternationals, but neither was in a Super Sport. Don Nicholson ran one of the engines in his white Impala Sport Coupe and Frank Sanders ran one in his red Biscayne sedan. Both engines were early production prototypes received directly from Chevrolet. These two 409s beat all comers with Sanders winning the Super Stock class in a race against Nicholson. Nicholson came back the next day and defeated Sanders for the Stock Eliminator title. Both of these 409 Chevys consistently ran the quarter mile in the low 13s at over 105 miles per hour.

Word of the 409's domination at the Winternationals set the NASCAR camps at Daytona buzzing. The Daytona 500 was just around the corner and Chevy fans were confident that the new 409 engine was the key to beating the dominant Pontiac and Ford teams. Unfortunately, the new 409 was only marginally faster than the previous year's 348s and the new 409 Chevrolets were never a threat on the Super Speedways. NASCAR's short track, where

Chevrolet History 1911–1955

The Chevrolet story began in March 1911, in a small shop on Grand River Avenue in Detroit, Michigan. There, a small group of men worked to assemble a five-passenger touring car named the Classic Six. The car's engine was designed by Louis Chevrolet, a famed race car driver of the era. These men were under the direction of William Durant, the financial genius who organized General Motors in 1908.

The Chevrolet Motor Company was incorporated on November 3, 1911. Durant leased a building on Detroit's West Grand Boulevard for the assembly of the new vehicles and 2,999 Chevrolets were produced during the first full year of operation. Durant chose the name Chevrolet because he found the name musical and liked the romance of its foreign origin. Also at that time, race car drivers were seen by the public as heroes, and naming a car after one couldn't hurt.

Durant was also responsible for the Chevrolet bow tie logo. In 1908, while visiting France, he was drawn to the design on the wallpaper in his room. The wallpaper's bow tie pattern marched off into infinity. Durant liked it so much he removed a sample from the wall and brought it home to show friends. He thought it would make a great logo for a car, and history has proven him correct.

In 1914, Chevrolet introduced a valve-in-head engine—an innovation that remains the basic principle of all automotive engines today. Also in 1914, additional assembly plants were opened and the sales organization was expanded. In 1915, electric lights became standard equipment. Chevrolet launched its bid into the low-price class with the 1916 introduction of the "490," so named because of its $490 price. Production in 1916 totaled 70,000 and the following year topped

125,000. It was also in 1917 that Chevrolet introduced its first V-8 engine. In 1918, Chevrolet became a part of General Motors and a new era of expansion began.

By 1924, Chevrolet had 6 assembly plants and 16 regional sales offices. The 1925 Chevrolet had a one-piece windshield with an automatic wiper on closed models. It also featured a single-plate clutch, 11-inch brakes, and a new banjo-type rear axle. Sales in 1925 topped 500,000. History was made in 1927 when Chevrolet sales topped one million, outselling Ford. Chevrolet didn't rest on its laurels, though, because in 1928 a new six-cylinder engine was designed and in 1929, Chevrolets could be purchased in several colors. Neither feature was available on the Model A Ford.

In 1934, Chevrolet introduced the "Knee-Action" suspension and the "Blue Flame" combustion chamber in its six-cylinder engine. In 1941, Chevrolet eliminated the running boards. Production that year was 1.3 million. Chevrolet ceased passenger car production on January 30, 1942, and from that date until October 3, 1945, Chevrolet plants built antiaircraft guns, shells, and Pratt & Whitney aircraft engines to support the war effort. Following the war, Chevrolet expanded production to meet the postwar boom.

In 1950, Chevrolet introduced the Bel Air hardtop and Powerglide transmission. Domestic production topped two million units. In 1953, the Corvette was introduced at the Motorama. Two years later, with the introduction of the 265-ci small-block engine and the smartly styled 1955 Chevrolets, Chevrolet established sales records and won the hearts of American car buyers. And, of course, the rest is history.

PREVIOUS PAGES

For 1962, Chevrolet restyled its full-size model; the only carry-over body components were the doors. The content of the Super Sport package also changed drastically. A lengthy list of high-performance options was no longer required to get the sporty SS trim on an Impala. Thin band white sidewall tires were now the only optional tires available, but they were not a required option with the Super Sport. A small tri-bar spinner was fitted to the center of a standard Impala full wheel cover, similar to the one on the 1961 model.

quick acceleration is required, favored the 409's shorter stroke design.

The 409 was intended to be available only in the Super Sport models in 1961. Chevrolet documentation confirms that 142 Chevys with the 409 engine were produced that year. Most of these vehicles went to racers or to lucky journalists for magazine road tests. Chevrolet received maximum return on its Impala SS press car investment. Several enthusiast

magazines gave the new 409 SS rave reviews. *Motor Trend* magazine tested a 409-powered 1961 Super Sport in its September 1961 issue. The *Motor Trend* Impala was driven with two different rear end ratios, 3.36 posi and 4.56 posi. With the 3.36:1 gears, the Impala SS ran the quarter in 15.31 seconds at 94.24 miles per hour. When they put in the 4.56:1 gears, the times dropped to 14.02 and the speed increased to 98.14. These were exceptionally good times for a full-size production car with a closed exhaust system and narrow bias-ply tires. The 1961 409 SS was a resounding success. It drew attention to Chevrolet's high-performance engine program and to the new Super Sport trim package. The introduction of the Super Sport option set the stage for 1962.

The basic body structure for the 1962 Chevy was the same as the 1961 model, and, in fact, the passenger doors and most of the body uppers were direct carryovers. A new front clip was added, along with revised quarter panels, deck lid, and full face bumpers. The Bel Air and Biscayne two-door sedans received a new roof, eliminating the flat-top design

The 1962 Impala preserved the six-taillight tradition that started in 1958. The bright rear panel on the Super Sport models had an engine-turned pattern. This effect was also used in the body side moldings. Above the right-hand set of taillights is a discreet Impala SS emblem.

of the 1961s. The 1962 Bel Air Sport Coupe retained the fastback roofline of the 1961 Impala Sport Coupe. The 1962 Impala Sport Coupe was given a new, more formal, cabriolet look with a roof that resembled a convertible top. Two creases were added across the rear portion of the roof. The side moldings were thinner and horizontal, giving the car a longer look. The rear was made to look wider by virtue of a large anodized aluminum panel. The grille was a simple egg-crate design. The front and rear bumpers had a much larger section, eliminating the painted valence panels below the bumpers on the 1961s. The front wheelhouses were now a full-skirt design, which protected the entire inside of the fender from road spray and corrosion.

Each of the three Chevrolet models—Biscayne, Bel Air, and Impala—had its own interior trim levels, with the Impala being the most plush. All full-size models had the same instrument panel as the 1961 Chevy, but the Impala's featured a standard clock and anodized aluminum trim. The 1962 Impala seats, like those on the 1961s, had a design pad sewn into them, but for 1962 this pad took the shape of "buttons and biscuits" in the seat backs. Once again, a small investment in foam and stitching greatly increased the appearance of the interior. The button-and-biscuit design was also carried into the Impala's door and quarter trim panels. Seven interior colors were coordinated with 14 solid exterior colors and 10 two-tone combinations.

For 1962, the Impala Super Sport option was reworked into a package that the average buyer found more attractive. Instead of the long list of mandatory options a customer was required to purchase in order to receive the Super Sport trim in 1961, the only requirement in 1962 was the purchase of a base Impala Sport Coupe or Convertible, after which the customer could then add the $156.05 Super Sport option. There were no engine requirements. The 1962 Super Sport Impala could even be ordered with a six-cylinder engine. A 1962 Impala Sport Coupe with the base 283 V-8 and the Super Sport option would list for approximately $2,680—a far cry from the 1961 SS price of nearly $4,000. This new lower price and the positive exposure that the 1961 SS received brought in many customers.

The 1962 Impala Super Sport offered a new level of trim that was more appropriate for a sporty car. The exciting news on the 1962 Super Sport interior was the addition of bucket seats. Bucket seats in a full-size car were first seen on the 1958 Thunderbird. In 1959, Pontiac became the first GM division to install them, but the 1962 Impala Super Sport marked the first time bucket seats were installed in a full-size

The new 327 was brought out in 1962 as a replacement for a lengthy list of 348-ci engines. It was offered in two horsepower levels, 250 or 300 (as shown). This 1962 Impala is equipped with air conditioning, power brakes, power steering, and even has an optional alternator. This was the first year an alternator was available on a Chevy; it would become a standard item in 1963, replacing the antiquated generator.

Chevy. Some members of Chevrolet's management worried (unnecessarily) that the Super Sport's bucket seat interior, with its five-passenger capacity, would be a detriment to selling a full-size car that had traditionally seated six. The bucket seats installed into the 1962 Super Sports were Corvair units, which were originally fabricated from a standard bench seat with the middle cut out. Pontiac was using the more luxurious Strato bucket seats, but they were too costly to be offered in a Chevrolet. Between the bucket seats was a small locking console. If a four-speed was optioned, a chrome console, similar to the one on the 1961 SS, was included. Three-speed manual and Powerglide-equipped 1962 Super Sports were column-shifted and did not have the floor console. The same passenger assist bar found in the 1961 Super Sport was fitted to the 1962 models.

The exterior featured tri-bar knock-off spinners on the center of the 1962's full wheel cover. Thin-line white sidewall tires, which were available only on the SS in 1961, were the only optional white sidewall tires available for 1962 Chevrolets. The Super Sports in 1962, unlike 1961, could also be ordered with black wall tires.

The full-length body side molding on base Impalas featured a color-keyed insert. On the Super Sport that insert was engine-turned. Engine turning (also called damascening) was a technique used on some of the finest motorcars in the 1920s and 1930s. The large rear panel that provided the background for the taillights was also engine-turned on the 1962 Super Sport. Finishing off the exterior were special SS quarter-panel emblems.

Along with exciting new styling, the 1962 Chevrolet Super Sport buyer was given a selection of six engines from which to choose. Anchoring the line-up was the 235-ci, 135-horsepower, six-cylinder engine. The base V-8 was the 170-horsepower 283. It was only available with a two-barrel carburetor and single exhaust. Both engines came standard with a column-shifted three-speed manual transmission. A three-speed overdrive or a Powerglide automatic was optional. The Powerglides used on the six and 283 were older versions with a cast-iron case, while Powerglides used on the new 327 had an aluminum case.

The 348-ci engine was no longer available in 1962. Replacing it were two new 327-ci engines rated at 250 and 300 horsepower. The 327 was based on the durable 283 small block design. Five years earlier, Chevrolet engineers came to the conclusion that 283 cubic inches would be the maximum displacement for the small block engine, but technological advances in metallurgy and casting allowed the engineers to increase the small block's displacement to 327 cubic inches by enlarging the bore by 1/8 inch and the stroke by 1/4 inch. This new combination easily produced as much power as the old 348, was more fuel-efficient, weighed 115 pounds less, and was less expensive to build and install because of the interchangeability of parts with the 283.

Externally, the 327 was the same package size as the 283. New blocks had to be cast to accommodate the increased bore and stroke. Extra material was added to the main bearing webs for strength, and the area around the cylinder bores was increased. The 327's crankshaft was forged and required machining of the block for counterweight

In 1962, Chevrolet offered the customer three selections in a passenger car: the full-size Biscayne, Bel Air, or Impala; the compact Corvair; or the new Chevy II. The Impala on the right is a Super Sport, complete with bucket seats and center console. Bucket seats were offered in the Corvair Monza and they could also be specified on certain Chevy II models, but neither of these cars offered an SS option. *Copyright 1978–1999 GM Corp. Used with permission of GM Media Archives*

clearance. The rods were the same as those used in the 283, although the beam section was beefed up. Pistons were cast flat-tops with machined reliefs for valve clearance. The 327's compression ratio was 10.5:1, necessitating premium fuel.

Cylinder heads for the 250-horsepower version of the 327 were similar in design to those used on the 283 engines, including the 1.72-inch-diameter intake valves and 1.50-inch-diameter exhaust valves. Both Carter WCFB and Rochester 4GC four-barrel carburetors were used with the 250-horsepower engine. The cylinder heads on the 300-horsepower 327 had larger ports and larger 1.94-inch-diameter intake valves. These same heads were also used on all 300-, 340-, and 360-horsepower Corvette 327 engines. A Carter AFB topped the 300-horsepower version of the 327. Although both engines were equipped with dual exhaust systems, the 300-horsepower engine was equipped with larger exhaust manifolds that had 2-1/2 inch outlets. Both engines came standard with a temperature-controlled fan. A column-shifted three-speed syncromesh transmission was standard, while aluminum-cased Powerglide and four-speed manual transmissions were optional. Overdrive was not an option for either of these engines and the infamous Turboglide transmission was discontinued.

The 327 was a magnificent addition to Chevrolet's catalogue of engines. At a list price of $83.95 for the 250-horsepower version and $137.75 for the 300, they were both bargains. Chevy customers agreed by purchasing a total of 240,909 optional 327 engines in 1962. This was four times the number of 348s sold in 1961.

At the top of Chevy's horsepower chart in 1962 were two 409s: a single four-barrel version rated at 380 horsepower and a dual-quad version rated at 409 horsepower. The higher horsepower ratings over the 1961 version came as a result of new head castings that featured larger ports and valves, new intake manifolds, and a new longer duration camshaft. All 409s came from the factory with dual head gaskets, which dropped the advertised compression ratio of 11.0:1 about one point for increased driveability. As a matter of course, serious racers would tear the engine down and rebuild it with a single head gasket to reclaim lost compression and power.

Dual four-barrel Carter AFBs were new for the 409 in 1962. "We started with three twos, but they were giving us balance problems," Dick Keinath recalls. "Maybe we couldn't get enough volumetric through three two-barrels. The vacuum linkage was not all it was supposed to be, either. Adding dual-fours was the natural thing to do, because we had

At the top of Chevy's performance engine list in 1962 was the 409. It was available in a single-quad version rated at 380 horsepower or a dual-quad version like this one, which was rated at 409 horsepower. This engine was visually distinguished by its scalloped valve covers.

experience with the Corvette. It was easier to handle with two carburetors and two linkages." The linkage used on the 409 was a progressive type, identical to the linkage used on the dual-quad Corvette engine. On this type of installation, the rear carburetor is the primary. Its front throttle bores are centrally located on the manifold, providing good fuel distribution to all cylinders at low speeds. The front carburetor is the secondary, opening for high speed operation only.

In the early 1960s, development of the 409 within Chevrolet was progressing at a feverish pace. Chevrolet's engineers were frustrated trying to draw additional horsepower out of the 409. "It was a very independent engine," Keinath says. "It wouldn't respond to the normal things you would do to get the volumetric efficiency higher—valves, porting, camshafts." Keinath admitted that they were a little spoiled by how easily horsepower could be drawn out of the small block. "It was a very frustrating experience for us," Keinath confesses. "We'd increase or decrease the overlap on the camshaft and it would not respond the same way as the small block. It was either skewed a little to one end or the other."

Both 409s came standard with a column-shifted three-speed manual transmission, but few were produced with that gear box. Most 409s were ordered with the optional close-ratio four-speed manual transmission. With the four-speed came a column-mounted Sun tachometer redlined at 6,200.

The 1962 409s picked up where the 1961s left off—winning races on the drag strip. Throughout the year, race-prepared 409s were running the quarter mile in 12.5 seconds at a speed of 112 miles per hour. Unfortunately the 409s did not fair as well on the NASCAR circuit. They were reliable, but didn't have the power in the longer runs to match the powerful 421 Pontiacs.

Overall, Chevrolet's racing success with the 409 in 1961, along with the positive press it received, built a great deal of enthusiasm for the 1962 models. By the time the 1962s were released, Chevrolet's Los Angeles Zone Office had back orders for more than 500 Super Sport 409s. In 1962, 8,909 Chevys were equipped with the 409 engine. The 409 was a great image builder and drew customers into the showrooms.

By looking at which performance options customers ordered on their 1962 Chevys, a definite performance trend could be seen. In 1961, only 7,073 full-size Chevys were equipped with four-speed transmissions. In 1962, that number more than tripled to 25,448. The same trend could be seen with the number of Positraction rear axles ordered. In 1961, Chevy sold 44,853 Positraction rear axles and in 1962 that figured ballooned to 74,257.

Chevrolet celebrated its Golden Anniversary in 1962. To commemorate the event, the company changed the color of the small bow tie insert on the hood and the deck lid emblem from blue to gold. Many dealers placed a fully loaded Super Sport Impala painted in the special Anniversary Gold color in the front of their showrooms. When delivering a new Chevy in 1962, the keys were on shiny brass key chains that said, "Thank you, America, for 50 years of confidence."

But giveaways were hardly needed to attract customers in 1962. The restyled Chevrolet body with its new roofline was enthusiastically received by the auto-buying public. The reduced price of the Super Sport option was also a big incentive for customers to upgrade from a standard Impala. So by year's end, of the 1.4 million full-size Chevys sold in 1962, just under 100,000 were Super Sports. Every enthusiast magazine that tested a Chevrolet in 1962 raved about it. The new Super Sport was so successful that

The popularity of drag racing was skyrocketing in the early 1960s. One of the fastest cars on the strip was the 409-powered Impala SS. At that time, a well-tuned 409 could run the quarter mile in 12.2 seconds at 115 miles per hour.

In 1963 the full-size Chevy was completely redesigned, carrying over only the two-door sport coupe's formal roof that was introduced in 1962. Its sheet metal was crisply detailed with several horizontal character lines, which made the car look longer.

the Ford product planners across town in Dearborn were working on the Galaxie 500XL, their own bucket-seated version to compete against the Super Sport in 1963.

The smartly restyled 1963 Chevrolet Impala was overshadowed by the release of the hot new Sting Ray. While many people were drawn into the showrooms to look at the Corvette, they ended up driving out in a sensible new Impala. But to get the sporty feel of a Sting Ray, many ordered the Super Sport option, along with one of the optional V-8 engines and a four-speed transmission.

Chevy designers succeeded in their annual challenge of making the new 1963 Impala look like a mini-Cadillac. The rooflines were carried over from the 1962 models, with the exception of the four-door hardtop. Below the belt line, the sheet metal was new and sharply creased. Two prominent horizontal character lines ran along the sides, which gave the 1963 Chevy the illusion of length. Along the lower of those two lines, Chevy designers added a thin molding to the Impala and Bel Air, enhancing this illusion of length. The Impala molding had a color-keyed insert that was replaced with an engine-turned insert

The lower body side molding was one of the styling cues that gave the 1963 Impala the look of a mini-Cadillac. This Impala SS is fitted with an optional grille guard and optional rocker panel moldings.

on the Super Sport. All 1963 Chevrolets received a new, straight A-pillar design, which reduced wind noise and provided a better seal for the windshield. The cowl and rocker panels were redesigned to allow fresh air to flow through the rockers, flushing out trapped water and reducing corrosion.

The front of the 1963 Chevy appeared wider and more massive, because of the enlarged grille opening. The grille was an egg-crate pattern executed in anodized aluminum. Below each pair of headlights was a small amber turn signal. This was the first year for amber turn signal lights, which were considered a safety item because they could be more easily seen against the glare of the headlights. Twin windsplits accented the Chevy's broad hood. The rear of the new Chevy Impala was coved

out with six circular taillights surrounded by an aluminum panel, which was engine-turned on the Super Sports. All other full-size models had only four taillights, with the body-color rear panel outlined with a thin aluminum molding.

The 1963 Impala's "Cadillac look" didn't come about by accident. When the 1963 Chevys were being designed, Chevrolet Chief Designer Clare MacKichan was home recuperating from a bad car accident. His assistant, Dave Holls—who had just transferred in from the Cadillac studio—was in charge of the Chevrolet studio and the exterior design of the 1963 Impala while MacKichan was absent. Holls kept MacKichan up-to-date during regular visits to his home. Much of the 1963 Chevy's "Cadillac look" could be attributed to Dave

Holls' experience in the Cadillac studio. "The 1963 Impala had a lot of Cadillac in it, with that low, color-accented body molding. And the front looked a little like a '61 Caddy," says Holls. "Because of the similarity, they used to kid me that the leopard didn't change its spots."

Chevrolet interiors, in 1963, received a fresh look, primarily because of a new instrument panel design. The new panel was a smooth, sweeping design that housed the instruments in a deep recess in front of the driver. The glove box returned to the right-hand side, in front of the passenger seat. Delco Electronics provided the optional tachometer that was housed in a well-integrated nacelle at the base of the steering column. Impala seats were covered in a combination of cloth and vinyl and the Super Sport models were trimmed in all vinyl. All Impala seat backs carried the "button-and-biscuit" pattern design pad.

As in 1962, the Super Sport option could only be specified on an Impala two-door Sport Coupe or Convertible. Bucket seats, now a standard fixture of the Super Sport option, were separated by a new, longer chrome console. All Super Sports in 1963 featured a console-mounted floor shift when an optional Powerglide or four-speed transmission was ordered. A passenger assist bar was no longer part of the SS trim. Super Sport exteriors featured the SS badges and engine-turned finish for both side molding and rear insert. Special three-bar spinner wheel covers rounded out the SS exterior trim.

Chevrolet announced several new production options in 1963. For $75.35, a vinyl roof covering, in white or black, could be ordered on the Impala Sport Coupe. A new seven-position Comfortilt steering wheel was available on all Bel Air and Impala series for $43.05. To specify it as an option, the customer was required to order power steering and a Powerglide or four-speed manual transmission. Introduced late in the model year was the AM/FM push-button radio. At $134.50, this new sound system was almost twice the cost of the AM push-button radio. Chevrolet offered a wide assortment of heavy-duty options for a very reasonable price. In 1963, an optional heavy-duty battery listed for only $7.55; a heavy-duty radiator listed for $10.80; 6-inch-

This is one of the more than 185,000 Impala SS models that rolled off the assembly line in 1964. The convertible top is covered to protect it during transport to the dealer. The special SS wheel covers were shipped in the trunk to be installed prior to delivery to an anxious customer. *Copyright 1978–1999 GM Corp. Used with permission of GM Media Archives*

wide wheels cost only $5.40; and the best bargain of all was the heavy-duty front and rear springs and shocks for only $4.85.

Any of Chevrolet's seven engines were available for a 1963 Super Sport. Anchoring the line-up was the 230-ci, 140-horsepower inline six. This all-new engine was long overdue. It was based on the design of the 1962 Chevy II's new six-cylinder engine, but with a larger bore. Externally, the new engine was inches smaller than the previous six, reducing the overall weight by 23 percent. Many components were interchangeable with the Chevy II's four- and six-cylinder engines. In 1963, the 283's horsepower was increased to 195. This improvement was accomplished with an increase in compression ratio to 9.25:1 and a revised camshaft. The two 327-ci small block V-8 engines for 1963 (250 and 300 horsepower) were carryovers from 1962. The 230-ci six and 283

came with a three-speed manual transmission. Optional were a three-speed manual overdrive or a Powerglide automatic.

In 1963, there were three 409 engines to choose from: two high-compression, high-horsepower versions and one detuned version. Horsepower ratings for the two solid lifter 409s were increased from 380 to 400 for the single four-barrel version and from 409 to 425 for the dual-quad powerhouse. This increase in power was due to a revised cam profile and more efficient exhaust manifolds. Added to the 409 line-up for 1963 was a tamer 340-horsepower version. This docile 409 had small-port cylinder heads and a cast-iron intake manifold with a Rochester 4GC four-barrel carburetor. The 340 had a mild hydraulic cam and a 10:1 compression ratio that required premium fuel. Like the other 409s, the 340 came standard with a three-speed manual transmission, though four-speed

Chevy dealers loved to place fully loaded models in the center of the showroom. This dealership has showcased two 1964 Super Sport Impalas. These highly optioned models provided talking points for the salesmen and would easily trigger an anxious customer's impulse to buy. The Super Sport in the foreground is equipped with an optional black vinyl top, which was first offered on an Impala in 1963. *Copyright 1978–1999 GM Corp. Used with permission of GM Media Archives*

manual and heavy-duty Powerglide transmissions were optional. While down on horsepower compared to its solid lifter brothers, the 340 had a solid 420 lb-ft of torque at 3,200 rpm. All 409s came dressed with chrome-plated valve covers, air cleaner, and fuel lines.

Two other engines saw limited racing service in 1963 Impalas, and they both struck fear in the hearts of the competition like a spring tornado through a Kansas trailer park. On the drag strip, the Z-11-optioned Chevys held court, and on the high banks of Daytona, the "Mystery 427" set new records. It looked like another excellent year for Chevrolet on the race tracks until General Motors agreed to abide by the AMA's 1957 ban on the support of organized racing. In January 1963, all General Motors racing programs ground to a halt.

The cars already in service would compete through the year without any support from the factory. But as high-performance parts supplies dwindled, so did the number of competitors racing Chevys. By 1964, almost all of the professionals had switched to other brands to remain competitive.

The 1963 Chevy's chassis was a direct carryover from the 1962 model. The only improvements were self-adjusting brakes and an alternator (Chevrolet called it a Delcotron) that replaced the generator. Other revisions were an extended-life exhaust system and extended lubrication intervals. Chevrolet also standardized the PCV (Positive Crankcase Ventilator) valve on all engines. This simple device cleared the crankcase of harmful gasses, thereby reducing air pollution and extending engine life. In 1963, General Motors extended the factory warranty

A 1964 Impala Super Sport was a driver's delight. It was available with engines ranging from the 140-horsepower six to a tire-smoking 425-horsepower 409 V-8. This wide range of engines and transmission selections came with a lengthy option list, allowing the customer to build the car of his or her dreams.

to 24 months or 24,000 miles. At this time Chevrolet was putting a significant amount of money into testing the durability of its cars. Prototype testing included a 36,000-mile endurance run. These tests were run at General Motors' Milford, Michigan, test track and at other GM facilities in Mesa, Arizona, and Pikes Peak, Colorado.

Car Life magazine tested two new Super Sports in its March 1963 issue. Both were hardtops, one equipped with a 250-horsepower 327 and the other with a 340-horsepower 409. *Car Life* was pleased with the performance and the fit and finish of both cars, but it dinged Chevy for the lack of a light on the console-mounted Powerglide shift lever. At night, selecting a gear was done entirely by feel. They also denounced the handling of the 327-powered model. The 409, which came with stiffer springs and 8.00x14 four-ply tires, handled better through the turns than the 327 model that had 7.50x14 tires and softer springs. The *Car Life* testers felt uncomfortable with the ride of the softly sprung 327.

In 1964, almost every manufacturer had a sporty, bucket-seated, full-size performance-image car. Ford had its Galaxie 500XL, Plymouth had its Sport Fury, Pontiac had the 2+2 Catalina and Grand Prix, Dodge offered its Polara, and Mercury manufactured its Marauder. Each of these cars was designed and marketed to compete with the success of Chevrolet's Impala Super Sport.

This success prompted Chevrolet's management to make the Super Sport a distinct model instead of an option to an Impala Sport Coupe or Convertible. Previous to 1964, designers working on the Super Sport option were restrained by cost from making any major changes. Only small alterations and additions, such as emblems, consoles, and bucket seats, were allowed. Any changes to the door and quarter trim panels were seen as too costly. In 1964, when the Super Sport was made into a unique model, Chevrolet designers were given more freedom to develop the car's contents. The Impala Super Sport's door and quarter trim panels were distinctively

In 1964, Chevrolet made the Super Sport Impala a distinct model instead of an option, which allowed Chevy's designers to put even more money into the car. The interior is one place where that money turned into additional trim. The 1964 Super Sport no longer had to share door and quarter trim panels with the Impala. These new panels, with their distinctive horizontal "Y" detailing and SS emblems, were first prototyped on one of Bunkie Knudsen's personal cars.

trimmed in a unique "Y" scheme and the seats featured a pleated design. The pattern for this interior came from the custom interior of Chevrolet General Manager Bunkie Knudsen's personal car in 1963.

In 1962 and 1963 the Super Sport exterior side moldings were identical to those on the Impala, with the exception of an engine-turned pattern insert replacing a painted insert. In 1964, Impala Super Sports were trimmed with a unique full-length body molding. Even though the content of the Super Sport package was enhanced, it still only cost $161 more than a standard Impala—the same as in 1963.

Exterior styling for the 1964 Impala Super Sport was more formal than the 1963 models. The opening for the egg-crate grille was enlarged to fully surround the headlights in a large, oval shape, The traditional circular taillights, three on each side, graced the rear. Carried over from 1963 were the doors and body uppers. To maintain a low cost, Chevrolet used very little chrome plating. Most of the exterior trim was anodized aluminum accented by stainless window surrounds and a few chrome-plated emblems.

Chassis design for the 1964 Chevy was the same basic layout that supported the 1958 Chevy, and though small improvements were made from year to year, Chevy's six-year-old design was now obsolete. It provided a smooth ride when going in a straight line, but when cornering, it lacked stability.

Chevrolet's engine and transmissions for the 1964 Super Sport were the same as in 1963. The base engine was the 230-ci six-cylinder. The tried-and-true 283 anchored the V-8s and two optional 327s were again available. In 1964, the base 283 and two 327 engines were installed in more than 75 percent of all full-size Chevys, but the 340-horsepower 409 was also an option. In an era of inexpensive fuel, the 340-horsepower 409 was an easy item to select when ordering a fully optioned Chevy.

The two high-performance 409s were identical to those offered in 1963, but in a decade of escalating horsepower, the 409s were left in the dust by Chrysler's new hemis and Ford's powerful 427 high-riser. Anyone who wanted to be competitive in auto racing was not running a Chevy in 1964. A few die-hards tried, but it would be years before Chevy would be in the winner's circle again. The lack of participation in organized racing did not affect overall sales, but sales of the 409 engine dropped to 8,684—a 50-percent decline from the previous year.

In 1964, Chevrolet changed the four-speed shift lever to include a reverse lock-out, similar to the one on the Corvette. Also available as new options in 1964 were a transistorized ignition for all 409 engines and a sport-styled steering wheel with a

simulated walnut trim. Safety equipment also became a priority, as seat belts became standard equipment, instead of just an option.

Chevrolet had an outstanding year in 1964. Sales for all its car lines totaled 2.3 million, which was half of GM's 4.6 million domestic production. In 1964, one out of every four vehicles sold in the United States was a Chevrolet. This level of sales allowed record dividends to be paid to holders of General Motors' common stock. The $4.45 a share dividend was an 11-percent increase over 1963. In total, General Motors paid $1.2 million in dividends—the largest dividend any company had ever paid.

The 1964 Impala Super Sport bucket seats had their origins in the Corvair Monza. Super Sport interiors were trimmed in all-vinyl—a luxury at the time. The instrument panel on the 1964 Impala was a carryover of the one used on the 1963 models. This one has outlets for factory air conditioning. The inlays on the instrument panel and center console have the machine-turned pattern.

When Chevy engineers designed the 1965 Chevrolet, they started with a clean sheet of paper. The entire body was more rounded than the geometrically styled 1964 model. The 1965 model featured a split grille with an argent-colored lower valence panel. Super Sport models featured thin wheel-opening trim and no side molding. Tri-bar full wheel covers were standard on the Super Sport. This convertible is fitted with optional wire wheel covers. *Jim Knight/Late Great Chevys*

Chapter 2
Impala SS 1965–1996
The Legend Grows

In 1965, Chevrolet took several bold steps forward with its full-size car. Born in 1958, the Impala and subsequent Impala Super Sport led the industry in styling and performance. Chevrolet's customers benefited from superb engine technology and low prices. Between 1958 and 1964, the full-size Chevrolet was always a work in progress with modest evolutionary steps in engineering and design. The buying public displayed its distaste for revolutionary changes when it rejected the small, rear-engined Corvair. Chevy's management team took a lesson from that experience and adopted only those changes to which the public had been previously exposed and which had been seen as true improvements, rather than just gimmicks. In 1965, an entirely new perimeter frame and suspension would be added to the full-size car. This chassis design was pioneered under the 1964 Chevelle. At new car introduction, the Impala's styling was a dramatic departure from the 1964 model, but the engine and transmission line-up was the same. By midyear, a powerful new engine and a new technically refined transmission would be introduced, as well as a new luxury model. In 1965, Chevrolet spoon-fed the car-buying public one of its greatest achievements—the new Impala. Success was to be written all over that car like graffiti on an inner city freeway overpass.

With the exception of a fastback roofline, the original exterior styling of the 1965 full-size Chevrolet was only a small evolutionary step beyond the design of the 1964 model. Bill Mitchell, head of General Motors Styling, and Chevrolet's General Manager Bunkie Knudsen approved the design, and work began.

As cars go, the original 1965 Chevy was an acceptable design that probably would have sold well. However, Irv Rybicki, Chevrolet's chief designer, was not content with the austere look of the original design. Under Rybicki's direction, an unauthorized, second design was initiated that would revolutionize the appearance of the Chevrolet. Done without the knowledge of Mitchell or Knudsen—something unheard of in Detroit's automotive corporate culture—the new design ran concurrent with the original, using the same upper body, but featured a dramatic new lower body. Emil Zowada was the designer responsible for the prominent rear fender form. The final element of the new body to be resolved was the front end, which from the side appeared to be too static. Chevrolet designer Henry Haga remedied the problem by putting a forward lean into the design. The front end of the 1965 Chevrolet departed from the traditional stacking of hood, grille, and bumper. Below the nose piece, the grille was divided by the slender blade bumper. Rybicki's design team created a new treatment for the 1965 Chevy that was far superior to the original. If the design had been unsuccessful, Rybicki's end run would have been the equivalent of corporate suicide.

The new design was presented to Mitchell and Knudsen. Corporate executives never like surprises, but both liked the new design. Knudsen liked it so much that he was willing to go to General Motors' Board of Directors to get it approved, even though the previous design had been approved and the historically conservative board was reluctant to make even minor changes to an ongoing program. Knudsen, who knew cars and marketing, built a strong case for Rybicki's new design and the board approved the change.

As the head of General Motors' design staff, Bill Mitchell ran a tight ship, and the thought of an underling creating a new design without his approval was the equivalent of treason. Rybicki should have been blindfolded and made to walk the plank. But Bill Mitchell also loved beautifully designed cars and he liked the new Chevrolet design Rybicki and his team had developed. So, in private, Mitchell carefully explained to Rybicki his feelings on surprises and warned him to never do it again.

The design criteria for the 1965 Chevy called for a longer, lower car. Curved side glass (first seen on the 1964 Chevelle) on the new body upper contributed to the sleek shape. But, installing curved glass was the least of the engineers' problems. The new pancake hood and multi-piece front bumper created a myriad of design and assembly problems

that needed to be sorted out. And even though the overall profile was lower, the trunk was required to have more depth than that of Ford's Galaxie.

Supporting Chevrolet's beautiful new body was a full-perimeter frame, which replaced the dated X-frame. An all-new coil-spring front and rear suspension was added. Similar to the Corvair's design, the front suspension featured a single bushing inner mount on the lower control arm, supported by a horizontal strut rod. The upper arm was a conventional A-frame design. In 1965, Chevrolet introduced its new "Wide Stance" design that increased the front tread by 2 inches and the rear by 3. The new Salisbury-type rear axle was borrowed from the Chevelle and was mounted with two lower control arms and one upper on the right side. Chevrolets equipped with any of the optional V-8s were given an additional upper control arm on the left side. Brakes were carryover Bendix-type

When the 1966 models were released, only small changes were made to the exterior. This 1966 Impala Super Sport features optional wire wheel covers and a black vinyl top. Super Sports could be ordered with any engine, including a six. The flags on the front fender indicate that this car is powered by a big block.

self-adjusters, but power assist and metallic linings were optional. The new frame no longer required the troublesome two-piece drive shaft required by the X-frame design.

When the new 1965 Chevys were introduced to the public in the fall of 1964, the powertrain line-up was almost the same as the previous year. The only exceptions were the resurrection of the four-barrel carbureted 220-horsepower 283 and the deletion of the 425-horsepower, dual-quad 409. Also interesting was the fact that all the V-8 engines could be ordered with a four-speed manual—even the two-barrel carbureted 195-horsepower 283. By midyear, the engine line-up changed dramatically when both 409s were dropped and two new 396-ci engines were added. The release of the new 396 engine generated as much excitement as Chevrolet's first V-8, 10 years earlier.

The design of the new 396-ci big-block engine was based on the Mystery 427 engine that debuted at the 1963 Daytona 500. Dick Keinath designed both the Mystery 427 and the 396. He originally designed the 396 with a 427-cubic-inch displacement that could easily be upped to 454. By reducing the 427's bore from 4.25 to 4.094, the cubic inch displacement dropped to 396.

As hard as they tried, Chevy engineers were never able to develop the 409. It never responded to the typical hot rodder's tricks of adding cam and carburetion like the small block. The lack of a configurable combustion chamber was one of its major drawbacks. The new big block engine would take the best features of the 409 and small block designs and add several other refinements. "We started [for the 396/427] with a clean sheet of paper," said Keinath. One improvement over the small block design was the elimination of siamesed exhaust valves (on cylinders 2&4 and 3&5). "The siamesed exhaust valves concentrated too much heat around those two valves," said Keinath. "Because of the excess heat, the valve seats would tilt, causing valve leakage and burning under extreme conditions—so I changed it." Keinath is also responsible for the canted valve design that was initially done to allow the use of larger valves. The key in allowing the valves to be tilted was the ball-stud rocker arm. Enthusiasts nicknamed this valve placement "porcupine" because of the way the rocker studs protruded from the head in several directions.

Two different 396s were offered in the 1965 Chevrolet passenger car: a 325-horsepower street version and a 425-horsepower version identical to the one offered in the Corvette. Both engines were similar in exterior appearance and had the same bore

In 1966, Chevrolet made a major change to the interior of its Super Sport model by replacing the old Corvair-based bucket seats with the new Strato buckets. These new seats didn't have the bulk of the previous buckets and for 1966 were available with optional headrests. The four small knobs on the center console control the optional stereo.

and stroke (4.094x3.76 inches), but internally they were very different. The 425-horsepower version had a forged crankshaft and pistons (11.0:1 compression), four-bolt main bearing caps, 2.19-inch-diameter intake valves, a long 336-degree duration solid lifter cam, and a large Holley carburetor on an aluminum intake manifold. All 425-horsepower engines were equipped with a standard transistorized ignition system. This magnetic pulse system was available at an extra cost on the 325-horsepower engine. Inside the 325-horsepower 396, the crankshaft and pistons (10.25:1 compression) were cast, the main bearing caps were attached with two bolts, and the camshaft profile was mild. A mixture of Holley and Rochester Quadrajet carburetors were used on a cast-iron intake manifold. All 425-horsepower 396 engines came standard with a dual exhaust system. The 325 engine came standard with a single exhaust system, but for an extra $21.05 the customer could add duals. The new 396 engines were enthusiastically received. In 1965, 57,292 full-size Chevys were optioned with one of the two 396 engines. To put that number in perspective, a total of only 37,465 full-size Chevys were sold with 409 engines between 1961 and 1965. The new 396 engine was the holy grail that Chevy enthusiasts had been searching for.

Also introduced when the 396 debuted was an entirely new automatic transmission—the three-speed Turbo Hydra-Matic 400. In 1965, the Turbo 400 was only available in full-size passenger cars optioned with the 325-horsepower 396. Its design—a three-element automatic, hydraulic torque converter with a compound planetary gear set—was based on the hearty Hydra-Matic transmissions that were used in Pontiacs and Oldsmobiles. The Turbo 400 was a perfect match for the powerful new 396 engine.

Production of the Impala Super Sport reached an all-time peak of 243,114 units in 1965. As in 1964, the Super Sport was a unique model available in either a four-passenger sport coupe or a convertible. Similar to the 1964 model, it could be purchased with a six-cylinder engine. But unlike the 1964 model, there was no full-length body side molding. Instead, the sides of the new SS were clean with a simple thin molding around each wheel opening. A Super Sport emblem was placed on the front fender just behind the front wheel opening. Super Sport emblems were also placed in the grille and on the trim panel at the rear deck lid opening. Unique tri-bar full wheel covers helped distinguish the Super Sport from the standard Impala. The interior featured vinyl-trimmed bucket seats and special door trim with SS inserts. The instrument panel on the Super Sport featured an aluminum insert that replaced the woodgrain insert seen on the Impala.

In 1965, the Super Sport lost its dominance at the top of the Chevrolet pyramid. It was replaced by the tony Caprice option. One morning while nosing around the Chevrolet studio, Bunkie Knudsen found sketches of a luxury design based on the Impala and done in response to Ford's upscale LTD. Knudsen liked the concept and asked to have the package installed on a 1964 Impala four-door hardtop as a prototype. When completed, this smartly trimmed black Impala became the mold for the 1965 midyear release of the Caprice. The name Caprice was coined by Bob Lund, Chevrolet's general sales manager, after a classy restaurant he frequented when in New York.

Selling Chevys in 1965 was almost as easy as giving away free cups of beer at a July baseball game. Sales records were set with 2.3 million cars sold—almost half of which were Impalas. Ford wasn't far behind with sales of 2.1 million. This was a 36-percent increase over Ford's 1964 sales, due in large part to the skyrocketing success of the sporty new Mustang.

Because of the success of the 1965 model, Chevrolet looked toward 1966 as another banner year. The 1966 model received a mild facelift and a few changes were made to the list of optional engines. General Motors' flagship division now had five full lines of cars to engineer, manufacture, and sell. Chevy's staff thrived on the challenge, and succeeded.

The full-size Chevrolet's basic body was carried over for 1966. New, more-upright end caps were added to the ends of the quarter panels, and the traditional Impala taillight arrangement featuring three circular taillights on each side was replaced with a rectangular three-segmented horizontal taillight that wrapped around the edge of the quarter panel between the end cap and the rear bumper. Up front, the leading edge of the fenders was also redesigned with a smooth, rounded shape. The egg-crate grille pattern on the 1966 Chevy was tightened up. Along the horizontal character line that ran the length of the car, Chevy designers ran a thin anodized aluminum molding that wrapped around the rear of the car. These changes gave the 1966 full-size Chevy a more formal and precise look.

Super Sports were again a separate Impala model in 1966, offered in both two-door sport coupe and convertible bodies. The exterior trim consisted of Super Sport script behind the wheel opening in the front fender and Impala SS emblems in the grille and on the rear of the deck lid. New tri-bar full

In 1965 Chevrolet dropped the 409 engine and released the 396 in two horsepower versions, 325 and 425. In 1966, Chevy introduced the 427. It was available in a 425-horsepower version and the 390-horsepower version pictured here. Both of these engines were identical to the ones installed in the Corvette.

wheel covers were also part of the Super Sport's exterior trim. The Super Sport's all-vinyl interior featured the new Strato bucket seats, a full-length chrome console, and an Impala SS emblem on the glove box door. New options for 1966 included a four speaker AM/FM stereo radio, a new gauge cluster, and tilt steering wheel. Once again, all Super Sport models were available with any engine and transmission combination, and the long list of factory options gave the customer plenty of ways to personalize a new 1966 Chevy Impala Super Sport.

In 1966, the Caprice replaced the Super Sport as the flagship of the Chevrolet line. No longer an option, the Caprice was now its own series and, for 1966, included an attractive two-door coupe and station wagon in addition to the four-door. This expansion to the spectrum of full-size Chevys may have been in response to the change in the auto-buying market. Younger buyers, not satisfied with oversized land yachts, were starting to opt for the emerging midsize performance cars, such as Chevy's hot SS396 Chevelle. Chevrolet's long-time customers were now in their salad days and wanted a more upscale, full-size car. The Caprice offered the luxury of a Pontiac or Oldsmobile with the price and reliability of a Chevy.

Mechanically, the 1966 Chevy was very similar to the 1965 model, with the exception of a few changes in the line-up of optional engines. A new 327-ci engine, rated at 275 horsepower, replaced the

250- and 300-horsepower versions that had been available since 1962. This 327 carried a mild hydraulic cam and a Rochester Quadrajet four-barrel carburetor. The 275-horsepower engine rested midway between the 220-horsepower 283 and the 325-horsepower 396.

At the upper end of the 1966 horsepower spectrum, two new 427-ci big-block engines were offered: a hydraulic cammed version rated at 390 horsepower and a solid lifter version that was underrated at 425 horsepower. Like all of Chevrolet's optional V-8s, the 390-horsepower 427 had a forged crankshaft, but the pistons were cast aluminum. The camshaft was a long-duration, with hydraulic lifters. A single Rochester Quadrajet carburetor was used on a cast-iron intake manifold. The 425-horsepower 427 (option L72) installed in the 1966 Chevy was very similar to the 425-horsepower 396 offered in 1965. To get 425 horsepower out of the 396 in 1965 it had to be revved to 6,400 rpm. The same horsepower rating was wrung out of the 427 at 5,600 rpm. Both engines were equipped with the same 336-degree duration camshaft. It's obvious that some number fudging was done at Chevrolet as to the true output of the 427.

The standard transmission for the 1966 Chevy was the three-speed manual or the heavy-duty three-speed when a 396 or 427 was optioned. An overdrive transmission was available with the six and both versions of the 283. A four-speed manual

The 1966 Impala's delicious styling is a result of a gamble taken by Henry Haga in the Chevrolet studios. It was under his direction that the 1965 Impala exterior took shape. The 1966 Impala was the first model since 1959 to not have six circular taillights, although each of the rectangular taillights was split into three segments. Copyright 1978–1999 GM Corp. Used with permission of GM Media Archives

was optional with all the V-8s. Close-ratio gears in the M22 four-speed were only available when the 425-horsepower 427 was ordered. The Powerglide was available on all engines up through, and including, the 325-horsepower 396. The Turbo Hydra-Matic 400 was also optional on that engine and on the 390-horsepower 427. The 425-horsepower engine did not have an automatic transmission option.

Sales were down for the entire automotive industry in 1966, with total sales of 8.8 million. Chevrolet had a good, but not great, year with sales of full-size Chevrolets dipping to 1.5 million (which equaled 1962 sales). The toughest pill for Chevrolet to swallow in 1966 was being outsold by Ford.

In 1967, the full-size Chevy received a complete facelift. The new body had the same lengthy fastback proportions as the previous two years, but now featured flared quarter panels and front fenders with crisply defined upper edges. Even though the new body appeared longer than its predecessor, it measured the same. The fastback roofline on the two-door hardtop looked even longer, as it extended to the leading edge of the deck lid without a filler panel in between. The elliptical wheel openings were enlarged slightly and the pancake hood was replaced with a traditional hood that slightly jutted out over the grille. In the rear, the taillights were again segmented three to a side. The blade bumpers of the 1965 and 1966 models were replaced with full-width chrome bumpers.

The engine line-up for 1967 was trimmed to two standard and three optional engines. The 155-horsepower six and the 195-horsepower 283 were the reliable base engines. Returning as optional engines were the 275-horsepower 327 and the 325-horsepower 396. New to the optional engine chart was a 385-horsepower 427. It was identical to the 390-horsepower engine in the 1967 Corvette except for the carburetion. The Corvette was fitted with a Holley but the passenger-car version used a Rochester Quadrajet. All of these optional engines were available in every full-size model.

In 1967, Chevrolet once again restyled the full-size body. The new design was accentuated by crisp character lines on the tops of the front fenders and rear quarters. The Super Sport option was offered on the Impala sport coupe and convertible. All 1967 Impala Super Sports had the vertical bars of the grille blacked out. This 1967 Impala SS convertible has optional simulated mag wheel covers. *Copyright 1978–1999 GM Corp. Used with permission of GM Media Archives*

In addition to the regular SS option to the Impala, Chevy also offered a special Super Sport in 1967—the SS427. The SS427 Impala was distinguished by a special domed hood, SS427 emblems in the center of the grille and on the deck lid, and unique flags, designating the 427 engine, on the front fenders. All SS427 models came standard with red stripe tires. Fifteen-inch Rally Wheels were specified when disc brakes were added.

Dropped from the list of optional engines was the 220-horsepower 283 and the 425-horsepower 427. In addition to the 396 and 427, the Turbo Hydra-Matic transmission was now available with the 327. Some documentation lists a 425-horsepower 427 as being available for the 1967 Chevrolet, but if indeed it was, it would have had to have been a COPO (Central Office Production Order) item.

To comply with federally mandated standards, 29 new or improved safety features were added to all 1967 Chevrolet passenger cars. An energy-absorbing steering column that had been in design and testing for five years was now standard equipment. Upon a frontal impact, this column was designed to collapse, rather than impale the driver, thus absorbing the energy of the collision. New door lock mechanisms were also installed to prevent the car doors from opening during an accident. Four-way hazard warning switches were installed on all Chevrolet steering columns and seat back latches were added to the folding front seat backs.

Chevrolet first installed disc brakes on the 1965

Corvette. Due to the Corvette's small production run, it was easy to test an entirely new braking system. It was on the Corvette that Chevy engineers gained experience with disc brake technology. In 1967, Chevrolet was ready to offer disc brakes as an option on all car lines except Corvair. Standard with the disc brake option were attractive 15-inch Rally Wheels. The stamped-steel wheels had five slots in the center web section and were painted argent silver. A small hubcap fit over the lugs and a trim ring was added to the outer rim. The simplicity of this wheel's design, combining form and function, has made it a classic.

Braking systems on every full-size Chevy were further enhanced with a dual master cylinder that split the braking system into two pairs of wheels (fronts and backs) to provide a degree of safety in the case of certain brake failures. Other safety-related items standard on all 1967 Chevys included two-speed windshield wipers with washers, back-up lights, padded sun visors, rear seat belts, a side-view mirror, and an antiglare interior rear-view mirror.

In 1967, Chevrolet revised its tactics on big car

sportiness and performance by offering two Super Sport versions. The basic Super Sport, available in two-door hardtop or convertible, featured Chevrolet's all-vinyl Strato bucket seat and SS trim upgrade to the Impala two-door hardtop or convertible. Exterior features of the Super Sport consisted of thin moldings that outlined the wheel openings and a rocker panel molding that extended behind the rear wheel opening to the rear bumper. Special SS wheel covers were part of the package. In response to federal safety regulations, they no longer featured the tri-bar flippers.

Available as an option to the 1967 Super Sport Impala was the SS427. This option was built around the 385-horsepower 427-ci engine. The SS427 had its own special exterior ornamentation. Most notable was the unique crossed flag emblem on the front fender with the numbers 427 above. Distinctive SS427 emblems were placed in the center of the blacked-out grille and at the lower edge of the deck lid. These emblems were similar in appearance and placement to those on the SS396 Chevelle. A special bodyside accent stripe was available only for the SS427-equipped Super Sports. All SS427s came with 8.25x14 red stripe tires, and those cars equipped with disc brakes received G70x15 red stripe tires. The most unmistakable item on the SS427 Impala was the special domed hood. The standard Chevy hood had a small peak that ran down the center, but the SS427's hood had a raised tapered blister in the center similar to the one on the small block Corvette. A chrome insert simulating three square carburetor intakes topped that blister. In 1967, General Motors' only vehicle with multiple carburetion was the Corvette. One can only imagine that the special hood, in combination with the 427 engine, was destined for the Corvette's tri-power.

As good looking as the 1967 Super Sport models were, the public's interest in full-size musclecars was waning. The extra cost of the full-size car was a

The 1967 Impala sport coupe had the most aggressive fastback roofline ever seen on an Impala. The SS427 was powered by a 385-horsepower big block engine, which had dual exhaust. Options on this SS427 include a vinyl top and rear bumper guards.

The 1967 SS427 Impala was trimmed with a distinct set of emblems that were completely different from those on the Impala SS. Fitted to the grille and deck lid were these unique SS427 emblems.

factor, and performance-oriented customers didn't like the extra weight of the large body and chassis. Sales in 1967 were good, but profits were down due in large part to the increased cost of materials, labor, and federally mandated safety and emission equipment.

The 1968 full-size Chevys received a major facelift in the form of new front sheet metal and bumpers. The new front end looked like an update of the 1965–1966 design with a pancake hood, blade bumper, and egg-crate grille that extended down to a silver-painted lower chin panel. Hidden windshield wipers were part of the new full-size Chevy's design. The rear was updated with a new full-width bumper that housed six horseshoe-shaped taillights with a small body-color rear valence panel below. New side marker lights were added to the front fenders and rear edge of the quarter panels, and the chrome housing for the front marker lights incorporated the engine's displacement designation.

New to the 1968 Impala line-up was the Impala Custom Coupe. The Custom Coupe used the formal roof from the two-door Caprice. Available as an option only on the Caprice were hidden headlights, which, when closed, enhanced the horizontal lines and gave the front a wide look.

Astro Ventilation was one of the new features available as an option on the Impala. This fresh air distribution system was standard on the Caprice and balanced front and rear passenger air distribution under all driving conditions. It worked by taking cool outside air in through the vented hood into the cowl. Ducts in the instrument panel distributed the air to two ball outlets and to two kick panel vents. Each outlet had a positive shutoff, so air flow could be controlled independently. The floor-mounted shifter for automatic transmission–equipped Super Sports was redesigned for 1968. The handle on the new design resembled an inverted "U." The release detent bar was located under the handle, where it was less apt to be accidentally depressed. This new shift handle was connected to the Powerglide or Turbo Hydra-Matic transmission by an enclosed cable that replaced the traditional linkage and gave the designers more freedom with interior design.

A 307-ci V-8 replaced the 283-ci V-8 engine as the base in the Chevrolet. To gain the additional displacement, this small-block V-8 kept the same bore as the 283 (3.825-inch diameter) and used the stroke of the 327 (3.25 inches). The 307 was rated at 200 horsepower and was available only with a two-barrel carburetor. The 307 came standard with a three-speed manual transmission and was available with an overdrive, four-speed manual, Powerglide, or Turbo Hydra-Matic. Two optional 327s were available in 1968: one rated at 250 horsepower and the other at 275.

Both the Impala SS and SS427 featured a center console trimmed in chrome and brushed aluminum. The four-speed shifter featured a reverse lock-out and shift pattern inlayed on the knob. The shift pattern was also duplicated on the console. *Copyright 1978–1999 GM Corp. Used with permission of GM Media Archives*

Both engines came standard with a three-speed manual transmission and optional with a four-speed manual, Powerglide, or Turbo Hydra-Matic. A new disposable oil filter was standard on all V-8s.

The Super Sport was demoted from its distinct model position in 1967 back to option status in 1968. Those selecting the SS option were delivered a car that was not as distinctive as in previous years. The exterior Super Sport emblems were smaller than ever and the full wheel covers were the same as those on a standard Impala. The interior was fitted with bucket seats and a full console. The Super Sport option (Z03) in 1968 was available on the Impala Sport Coupe and Convertible. It was not listed as being available on the new Impala Custom Coupe. As before, the Super Sport could be ordered with any engine, even the six, though convertibles were required to be equipped with at least the base 307 V-8. The SS427 option that featured the 385-horsepower 427 was again available. The 1968 version featured the same style SS427 grille and trunk emblems. The unique hood featured transverse vents. Behind the front wheel openings were three

thin vertical louvers. All SS427s were equipped with G70x15 red stripe tires.

Chevrolet's design and engineering staff had been working overtime to produce the 1968 Chevy car line, which included new designs for the Corvette, Chevelle, and Nova, as well as many redesigned components for existing vehicles that were required by new federal regulations. With all this work, it's amazing that the full-size Chevy received any attention at all. Total passenger car sales for Chevrolet in 1968 reached 2.2 million, with 1.2 million of those being the full-size Chevrolet. But sales of the Super Sport continued to decline, and the end of the Super Sport Impala was near.

In 1969, the full-size Chevy was the only car in Chevrolet's line-up to receive significant exterior changes. The full-size Chevy was based on the same platform as the 1968 model. The major facelift included a new front-end treatment, revised fender and quarter panel shape, and two distinct rooflines on the two-door sport coupe models.

The Impala Sport Coupe now had a semi-fastback roof with much less slope than that of the 1968

In 1968, Chevy performed a facelift on the full-size models. The front end was restyled in a layer cake fashion, by vertically stacking a grille piece, the bumper, another grille piece, and the lower valence panel. In the rear, there was a small valence panel below the bumper. Super Sport and SS427 were options on Impala Sport Coupes and convertibles in 1968. *Copyright 1978–1999 GM Corp. Used with permission of GM Media Archives*

41

Sales of full-size Super Sports had been on the decline when Chevy introduced the 1969 models. The customer base for the full-size vehicles had been shifting to cars with more comfort. The 1969 SS was Chevy's last attempt to sell a large performance sedan. It was equipped with a 385-horsepower 427.

model. The Impala Custom Coupe and Caprice had a roofline that was more upright, featuring a unique concave rear window and C-pillar extensions that blended into the top of the quarter panel. The 1969 Chevy's front end was aggressively restyled with a chrome halo bumper surrounding the traditional egg-crate grille. Its design was reminiscent of the 1968 Pontiac LeMans without the vertical center bar. Recessed into the bumper was the new grille assembly, now constructed of chrome-plated plastic, which actually appeared richer than the previous anodized aluminum grilles. By using argent paint on different portions of the grille, several unique looks were created for various models. On the Super Sport models, the vertical bars were painted, leaving only the bright horizontal bars visible. Hidden headlights were again optional on the Caprice, but not on the Impala models. By sheer coincidence, the halo bumper front-end design also appeared on the Chrysler 300 in 1969. The rear end design of the 1969 full-size Chevy featured a full-width bumper with inset taillights and a small lower valence panel that was similar to the 1968 model.

The body sides of the 1969 full-size Chevys were a rather simple design, which blended well with the front and rear design. To retain the inner wheelhouses, the wheel opening cut lines were the same as those on the 1968 model. Subtle blisters were added to the surfaces around the front and rear wheel openings.

Chevrolet severely reduced the scope of the Super Sport in 1969 so that only an SS427 option was available on the sport coupe, custom coupe, and the convertible. Exterior markings consisted of SS emblems in the grille, on the deck lid, and on the sides of the front fenders. The only SS interior identification was on the center of the steering wheel. Bench seats were standard with the SS option—cloth in the coupes and vinyl in the convertibles. All-vinyl Strato bucket seats were an option. Front seats were now equipped with standard driver and passenger headrests.

Disc brakes were a required option on the full-size Chevrolets with the SS427 option. A new second-generation disc brake design was introduced for the full-size Chevy in 1969. This new design featured a large single piston with a floating caliper. A new dual-circuit master cylinder with larger reservoirs was added to handle the increased fluid volume. New brake rotors were also part of the package and

Rochester Quadrajet

In 1965, something new appeared on top of Chevrolet engines—the Rochester Quadrajet (also known as Q-jet) carburetor. At the time, this new four-barrel was the most advanced in carburetion to date. Chevrolet's first use of a four-barrel was in 1955 atop the then-new 265-ci V-8. That carburetor was a Carter WCFB (Will Carter Four Barrel)—the world's first four-barrel carburetor, which had been in production since 1952. By the mid-1960s, the WCFB was archaic. On Chevys, it had been superseded by the Rochester-built 4GC, but on Chevy's high-performance engines, the carburetors of choice were the Carter AFB and a wide variety of large Holley four-barrels.

The new Rochester Quadrajet had top-end breathing efficiency that was nearly equal to an all-out racing carburetor, but at low speeds, its fuel metering, atomization, and idle were equal to any small two-barrel. The secret of its success was the use of a pair of very small primary venturis (2.4 square inches) and two very large secondary venturis (7 square inches). The linkage between the primary and secondary was mechanical. The secondary throttles started to open when the primary side was two-thirds open. Secondary air flow was controlled by air valves that were tilted open by dynamic air pressure instead of throttle position. At full throttle, these air valves opened gradually between 2,000 and 4,000 rpm, and the gradual opening produced a continual varying venturi area that adjusted automatically to the engine's need for air, which resulted in a smooth transition between primary and secondary.

The Rochester Q-jet was first installed in 1965, on the 325-horsepower 396-ci engine. Throughout the musclecar era, Quadrajet carburetors were installed on most of the 396, 427, and 454 low- and medium-performance engines and almost every 327 and 350. During this time, many of the Quadrajets were built under license by Carter Carburetor Company.

The Rochester Quadrajet carburetor first appeared on the 1965 325-horsepower 396. Within a year, it became Chevy's standard four-barrel carburetor, replaced by a Holley only on the highest-performance engines. The Q-jet, as it was often called, offered excellent low-speed driveability and large secondary bores for high-speed operation.

In 1994, the Impala SS name and performance heritage was resurrected. Based on a police package Caprice and available only in black, the car was an instant success. In 1995 the Impala SS returned to critical acclaim with two added exterior colors. Copyright 1978–1999 GM Corp. Used with permission of GM Media Archives

the ones specified on the full-size Chevy measured 11.75 inches in diameter and 1.25 inches thick. A 15x6-inch wheel rim of conventional construction was specified with the disc brake option and 15-inch Rally Wheels were optional.

In 1969, the Super Sport option once again meant performance. The only power plants available were two 427-ci engines: the hydraulic lifter 390-horsepower version or the solid lifter 425-horsepower freight train. The 425-horsepower version was available with the Turbo Hydra-Matic 400.

Safety was an even bigger concern in 1969, and the new Chevy had several design changes. One of these was side impact bars, designed to reduce passenger injury. The bars were a welded-steel, two-piece construction that formed a box section. They were installed within the door and extended from the lock pillar to the hinge pillar. Another safety feature, automatic-locking front seat belt retractors were now standard on all Chevrolets.

In an attempt to reduce vehicle thefts, Chevrolet moved the ignition switch to the steering column. When the key was removed, it locked the ignition system, steering wheel, and transmission. Another antitheft feature was the relocation of the interior door lock knobs 12 inches forward from the rear edge of the door. The new location made access easier for driver and passenger and created an obstacle for anyone trying to jimmy the door open from the outside.

A new variable-ratio power steering unit was introduced in 1969, offering the driver faster, more responsive steering with fewer turns lock-to-lock and enhanced "road feel" in the straight-ahead position. A new high-pressure power steering pump was required for the system.

When the curtain came down on the Super Sport Impala in 1969, few tears were shed. Buyers who had been the early adopters of the Super Sport's performance image in 1961 and 1962 were now raising families and buying Caprices or station wagons, while those of us who never grew up were driving Chevelles or Corvettes. The Impala Super Sport had had a good nine-year run, and it was time for it to retire.

There was no Impala Super Sport model in 1970. In fact, the Impala name would soon fade from the memory of Chevrolet buyers, replaced by Caprice. It would be another 25 years before there would be another Impala or Impala SS. And this time, it would be on a four-door model.

Chevrolet restyled the Caprice for the 1991 model year. The sleek new Caprice replaced the boxy version that had been in production for several years and was well accepted by the buying public. The exterior of the new Caprice was so radically different that consumers initially shied away. Its rounded shape had been compared to a watermelon seed or an M&M candy, but the new design did its job aerodynamically by allowing the car to go faster with the same drivetrain.

One of the complaints about the 1991 Caprice was that the small rear wheel openings made the rear of the car look chubby. In 1993 Chevrolet opened them up and the car took on a more dramatic look. It was also at this time that Chevy was making aggressive moves under the skin: Chevy's 1993 police package Caprice was powered by a 210-horsepower, 350-ci V-8 and included a heavy-duty radiator, heavy-duty suspension, and antilock brakes. Police package Caprices could also be ordered with bucket seats. The plans for the 1994 police package included the 260-horsepower LT1 engine. Everything was in place for Chevy to make a high-performance touring sedan that would rival any upscale German import. The Caprice was about to spawn a bad-boy son and all it needed was a name and a little refinement.

For the name, Chevy reached back into the past for a name that would conjure up memories of performance and luxury. A name that would be readily identifiable to anyone who turned 16 between 1960 and 1969. There was only one choice—Impala SS.

The refinement of the 1994 Impala SS came in the way of gray leather-covered bucket seats and steering wheel. The standard 1994 Caprice wood-grain interior trim was replaced with satin black. There was a console, but gear selection for the four-speed automatic remained on the column. Other comfort and convenience features included dual air bags, AM/FM stereo cassette, air conditioning, power brakes, power steering, tilt wheel, remote trunk release, power door locks, power driver's seat, intermittent wipers, and power mirrors.

There was only one color choice in 1994—black. In addition, much of the side trim was also painted black to match. The quarter panel displayed a discreet body-color Impala SS badge. The new SS sat low on 17x8.5-inch, five-spoke alloy wheels. The only tire available was the P255/50ZR-17 BF-Goodrich Comp T/A. The Impala SS rode on a decidedly stiffer suspension than the Caprice. Visible through the wheel spokes, front and rear, were the 12.1-inch-diameter vented brake rotors. Applying the pressure to those brakes was Delco's latest ABS VI system. Larger antiroll bars and quick-ratio steering rounded out the package.

With one kiss on the cheek, Chevrolet transformed the frog-like Caprice into a prince of a car. The new SS Impala had enough acceleration to warm the heart of any Super Sport lover. *Motor Trend* magazine tested a new Impala Super Sport in its June 1994 edition. It ran from 0 to 60 in 7.1 seconds and ran the quarter mile in 15.4 seconds with a terminal speed of 91.1 miles per hour. Thirty-three years earlier, the then-new 409-powered 1961 Impala Super Sport tripped the same quarter-mile clocks in 15.31 seconds at 94.24 miles per hour. But,

to be fair, the 1961 model was 1,000 pounds lighter and didn't offer anywhere near the comfort or drive-ability of the 1994 version. The 1994 model excelled in braking, due in great part to the excellent brakes Chevrolet had developed for police pursuit use. From 60 miles per hour, it took only 120 feet to come to a halt. In 1961, the 120-foot mark was where the old-style drum brakes would initiate their fade routine.

Motor Trend loved the 1994 Impala SS. They said, "The Impala SS is as great a value as it is a performance statement. Your $23,355 [price as tested] buys the right engine, ride, and performance. And best of all, it ain't Your Dad's Car . . ."

The 1994 Impala was one of the few cars in history to become an instant collector car. Requirements for that exclusive club are low production numbers, good styling, excellent engine, the first year of production, and performance that matches the appearance.

Thankfully, Chevy didn't disappoint the Impala SS fans in 1995, and once again offered the model with few changes. The most noticeable change was the addition of two colors: Dark Cherry and Dark Green-Grey. In 1996, Chevy made two welcome additions to the package, a floor shift and a tachometer. Unfortunately, just when Chevrolet finally got it all right, it pulled the plug on the program. On May 17, 1995, *USA Today* reported the bad news in an article titled "GM Scraps Big Cars." The Arlington, Texas, plant that produced the Caprice and Impala SS would be converted to manufacturing highly profitable trucks. The last car would roll off on December 13, 1996. Because of the popularity of the police package Caprice, many law enforcement agencies wrote Chevrolet requesting that they not stop production. In an effort to appease the waiting market, Chevrolet produced an additional 25,000 police package Caprices in 1996.

An interesting sidenote to the demise of the 1996 Caprice was the effort of RCI, Inc., a Michigan-based company that outfits police cars. RCI wanted to buy the tooling for the Caprice, because it wanted to continue production of the popular sedan at a factory in Canada. General Motors refused, and the Caprice and Impala SS were laid to rest.

Chevrolet released a new front-wheel-drive Impala for the 2000 model year. As of yet, there has been no announcement that there will be an SS model. The 2000 Impala hasn't tugged at the enthusiasts' heart strings like the original Impala or even the reborn 1994–1996 models. If Chevy does decide to produce an SS model, it will have some awfully big shoes to fill.

When the 1964 Nova Super Sport was released, very little of the exterior was changed. Fourteen-inch wheels were standard with the SS option and the 1963 Impala Super Sport wheel covers were added. There had always been room for a V-8 in the Chevy II's engine compartment, and Chevrolet finally added one to the option list. *Chris Richardson*

Chapter 3

Chevy II Nova SS
Chevy's Small Car With Big Performance

Motor Trend magazine reported in June 1961 that Chevrolet was working on a new class of automobile intended to fill the gap between the full-size Chevrolet and the recently introduced compact Corvair. This new car was to be powered by a four-cylinder engine, have a 115-inch wheelbase, and have single-leaf springs supporting the rear axle. Codes for new cars are common in Detroit's automotive centers and *Motor Trend* reported that the code name of this new Chevrolet was H-35, usually shortened to just "H." In the fall of 1961, Chevrolet introduced the "H" car to the public as the 1962 Chevy II.

At that time, Chevrolet's Corvair was being outsold by the more conventionally designed Ford Falcon. The new Chevy II compared to the Falcon in roominess, body construction, engine size, and conventional drive-line layout. It was also important to overcome the Corvair's lack of luggage space and cramped interior. The new Chevy II was to have maximum interior package size with a clean, crisply styled exterior. The overall goal for the new Chevy II was to provide the American family with transportation at a reasonable cost. It was to be inexpensive to purchase, economical to operate, and easy to maintain.

The new Chevy II's body was constructed differently than any other Chevy to date. It was a remarkable piece of engineering and no expense was spared in its design and construction. The new Chevy II body consisted of two unitized assemblies bolted together at the cowl. (Chevrolet's first unitized car was the 1960 Corvair.) The design of the passenger compartment featured sturdy box sections in the roof rails and a double cowl. For durability, the underbody components were zinc coated prior to priming and sealing. The Chevy II's front-end structure was a welded assembly of front rails, fender aprons, radiator support, and cross members. This assembly was bolted to the passenger compartment in four locations with 14 bolts. Chevrolet was not the first to use a design in which two major body assemblies are bolted together; it was first seen on the Cord. The benefits of two-piece body construction were ease of manufacture and improved serviceability. There was a penalty in total vehicle weight, but the overall benefits of this design outweighed the small increase in weight.

Chevrolet designers created an outstanding exterior design that was trim and well proportioned. The new Chevy II didn't look like a scaled-down 1962 Impala, but had a look all its own. A strong character line ran the length of the car from the headlight to a peak in the quarter panel at the taillight. This styling cue would be seen the following year on the full-size Chevys. Chevy designers also put a lot of effort into the detail work around the wheel openings and rocker panel. The strong horizontal lines gave the new little car the illusion of length. Up front, the traditional egg-crate grille featured single headlights, while the rear of the car featured a slight cove with a single small taillight on each side. The front and rear bumpers were simple face bars with a slight wraparound on the ends. These bumpers were well integrated into the design of the front fenders and quarter panels.

The Chevy II's suspension was a combination of a high-mounted coil spring independent front

When Chevrolet introduced the Chevy II in 1962, the company offered bucket seats, but no SS option. For 1963, a Super Sport option was available on the Nova 400 Sport Coupe and convertible. *Copyright 1978–1999 GM Corp. Used with permission of GM Media Archives*

suspension and two single-leaf springs in the rear. The front springs were mounted on top of the upper control arm, which allowed the load to be more evenly distributed throughout the unitized front structure. The well-designed front suspension streamlined the front-end alignment process. Toe-in was adjusted by a threaded strut rod, and caster was adjusted with bushings fitted with eccentric washers, which eliminated the need for shim packs. Front sway bars were not part of the new Chevy II's suspension design.

The rear suspension was supported by a pair of parallel, single-leaf springs called Mono-Plate springs. Criticized by some as being unsafe, the Chevy II's single-leaf design was effective and proved to be as safe as any multi-leaf rear spring. The differential was a drop-out design similar to the rear axle design used on the full-size Chevys. Spring rates for both front and rear were relatively soft to sustain a smooth ride. Thirteen-inch-diameter wheels were standard with either 6.00 or 6.50 size tires, depending on the model.

Two brand-new engines were available for the Chevy II. A new 153-ci, 90-horsepower inline four-cylinder engine, and a new 194-ci, 120-horsepower inline six-cylinder engine were available. These two new engines shared many internal components,

which reduced manufacturing costs. A newly installed, automated line machined the blocks for both engines. Both of these blocks featured a bulkhead on each side of every connecting rod, which produced a very sturdy block with five main bearings in the four-cylinder and seven main bearings in the six-cylinder. The cylinder head design for both engines was similar to the heads on the small block V-8. They used a wedge-shaped combustion chamber, stamped rocker arms with pressed-in studs, and hollow push rods to carry oil to the valve train. A single-barrel down draft carburetor was used for both engines.

A column-shifted three-speed manual and a Powerglide were the only two transmissions offered in the Chevy II. The manual transmission was essentially the same as the one in the full-size cars, and the optional Powerglide was similar to the Powerglide offered in the Corvette. It was air-cooled and the outer surface of the torque converter housing had air scoops to increase cooling air flow.

The 1962 Chevy II was offered in a full range of body styles. The 100 and 300 series offered a two-door sedan, a four-door sedan, and a four-door station wagon. The deluxe 400 Nova series offered a two-door sport coupe, a two-door convertible and a four-door station wagon. The two-door sport coupe featured thin angular C-pillars, which also enhanced the illusion of length.

Chevy's new little economy car had an extensive list of options. Power steering and brakes were offered, but because of the light weight of the car, neither was needed. A long list of heavy-duty chassis components included metallic brakes for $37.70. The best bargain was the heavy-duty springs and shocks, priced at a whopping $4.90. The convertible did not have a power top, but the top's spring-loaded mechanism was well engineered and allowed one person to easily raise or lower it. No Super Sport version of the Chevy II was available in 1962, but for $69.95, bucket seats were optional on the Nova two-door Sport Coupe and Convertible.

In 1962, *Car Life* magazine thoroughly tested several different 1962 Chevy II models and all received high praise. The magazine's only recommendation to a prospective owner was to order the optional six-cylinder engine. *Car Life* magazine liked the car so well, it awarded the Chevy II its 1962 Engineering Excellence Award. In the article the testers wrote, "We think it represents a return to sensibility in terms of basic transportation."

Chevrolet had the foresight to initially engineer the Chevy II with enough room to accept a V-8 without any major modifications. The first V-8 installations didn't come out of the hot rod world, but straight from Chevrolet. At that time, Ed Cole was Chevrolet's general manager. He loved performance, and was the one responsible for plugging the little V-8 into the Nova. Harry Barr, his chief engineer, said, "You can't do that, Ed, that car will be so fast it will be dangerous." Ed's reply was, "That's what I always wanted—a car that was too fast for me to drive." The first Chevy IIs barely made it off the assembly line when Chevrolet's engineering team developed and made available a complete kit to install a small block V-8. Both *Hot Rod* and *Motor Trend* magazines in their March 1962 issues detailed the installation of a small block using over-the-counter Chevy parts in kit form, which included a new radiator, metallic brakes, a floor extension for the four-speed shifter, and molded radiator hoses. In 1962, the local Chevy dealer was the place to find some of the best speed equipment at the lowest prices.

The V-8-powered Chevy II would be the ultimate sleeper, able to fool any young Turk on the street into thinking that the driver of the docile-appearing Chevy II in the next lane was someone on the way to the grocery store in his dad's car. Drag racer Don Nicholson took a 360-horsepower fuel-injected 327 Chevy II station wagon to the 1962 Winternationals. There, he easily won the B Factory

Solid engineering and simplicity were hallmarks of the Chevy II Nova's design. Chevy designers took the time to carefully detail the Nova's body sheet metal and chrome trim. Amber turn signal lenses became standard in 1963, allowing them to be seen more easily against the glare of headlights. *Chris Richardson*

Experimental class. Nicholson's Chevy II wagon ran the quarter mile as fast as the 400-plus-cubic-inch super stockers.

The 1963 Chevy II line-up remained unchanged from the 1962 models. Minor trim changes barely distinguished the 1963 models from the 1962 models, which was unusual in an era where yearly styling changes were as common as the New York Yankees winning the pennant. Small engineering changes were made to the Chevy II to improve quality and durability. Like all the other 1963 Chevy car lines, the Chevy II had standard self-adjusting brakes and a Delcotron alternator.

In 1963, Chevy's product planners saw the light and added the Super Sport option to the Chevy II. This option was only available on the Nova 400 Sport Coupe and Convertible. For a list price of $161.40, the customer received a sporty exterior and an interior package that was similar to the one available with the Impala SS. The interior featured bucket seats, special instrumentation, and a console. If the optional Powerglide transmission was specified, a floor-mounted shifter was included. The exterior of the 1963 Chevy II Nova Super Sport was distinguished by a bright metal body molding that ran along the belt line. Silver paint was added to the body side molding and into the rear cove, and special Nova SS emblems

Nova interiors, even on the Super Sport, were Spartan. In 1964, the bucket seats were the same ones used in the Corvair and Impala. When a Super Sport was optioned with a Powerglide, a floor shift was standard. *Chris Richardson*

were added. Fourteen-inch wheels were now optional on all models and were required with the Super Sport option. Fitted to those wheels were the same tri-bar spinners as on the 1963 Impala Super Sport. In 1963, the Nova Super Sport option was popular, but unfortunately, General Motors divorced itself from all types of racing, and put a halt to any further development of high-performance packages. Had Chevrolet provided a V-8 for the 1963 Chevy II, sales would have probably been even better. This problem would be addressed again in 1964.

For 1964, the Chevy Nova once again remained essentially unchanged from the previous year. Enthusiasts could take heart that Chevrolet had not forgotten the performance level of its newest car, however, as the option list for 1964 finally included the 283-ci V-8 and a four-speed manual transmission. Unfortunately, the only 283 offered was the two-barrel version rated at 195 horsepower. But just when things started looking up for the Chevy II, Chevrolet reversed course by eliminating the sport coupe and convertible. Along with the demise of those models went the Super Sport. Possibly someone at Chevrolet felt that the Chevy II Sport Coupe

The 1965 Chevy II Nova was the final year of the original body style that debuted in 1962. Nova SS emblems were placed on the rear edge of the deck lid and on the quarter panels. The wheel covers are borrowed from the 1964 Impala SS. The Nova took on full musclecar status in 1965, with the availability of the optional 250- and 300-horsepower 327 engines. *Copyright 1978–1999 GM Corp. Used with permission of GM Media Archives*

and convertible provided too much internal competition against the new Malibu. It wasn't long before Chevrolet reversed course again and reinstated the sport coupe and the Nova Super Sport (as a separate model), but the convertible was history.

The 1964 Chevy II Nova Super Sport looked exactly like and was outfitted the same as the 1963 model, except for the deletion of the body side molding. The true excitement in 1964 was the addition of the 283 and a four-speed transmission. The 1964 Nova Super Sport was a bargain, with a base price of only $2,433. Add the 283 engine for $107, and the four-speed for an additional $188 and driving excitement could be had for as little as $2,728.

In the June 1964 issue of *Motor Trend*, a new V-8 Nova Super Sport was road tested. The car the editors selected was fully loaded with power steering, power brakes, air conditioning, and a sticker price of $3,503. Though heavily laden, the Nova Super Sport proved itself well, running the quarter mile in 18.0 seconds at a speed of 75 miles per hour.

The 1965 Chevy II was available in three series: the base 100, the upgraded Nova, and the top-of-the-line Nova Super Sport. All three series had the same sheet metal first offered in 1962. The only major modification to the 1965 Chevy II's appearance was a new grille and headlight trim up front. New larger taillights and exterior ornamentation was added to the rear. Eight two-tone colors were available on the 1965 Chevy II, along with 15 solid colors, of which 13 were brand new shades. Three colors, Evening Orchid, Crocus Yellow, and Glacier Gray, were only available on the Super Sport. Available as an option on the 1965 Chevy II was an AM/FM stereo radio.

In 1965, the musclecar race was under way, and Chevrolet was trailing by several laps. Chevy's quick fix to the problem was to slip the 327 into the Chevy II's engine bay. Both the 300- and 250-horsepower versions were available. They were backed by a standard three-speed manual, optional Powerglide, or optional four-speed manual transmission. The power-to-weight ratio of a Chevy II with the optional 300-horsepower engine was equal to that of a Pontiac GTO—but it cost hundreds of dollars less.

With all of the benefits offered in the 1965 Chevy IIs, they should have sold like crazy. But, they didn't. There were only 122,698 Chevy IIs sold

Chevrolet completely restyled the Chevy II Nova for 1966. The two-door sport coupes were elegant and well detailed. Super Sport models in 1966 used the 1965 Chevelle SS wheel covers. This 1966 peek-a-boo show display has a new Nova SS on hydraulic lifts that raise and lower the body, revealing the 283 V-8 and driveline. *Copyright 1978–1999 GM Corp. Used with permission of GM Media Archives*

in 1965—68,993 units *fewer* than in 1964. This was at a time when 1965 Impalas and Chevelles were selling at a record pace. The decline was particularly embarrassing for Chevrolet, since Chevy II's sales were barely half of its main competition, the Ford Falcon. Two major factors that contributed to the Chevy II's declining sales were dated styling and Chevrolet's other new midsize, the Chevelle. During a press conference at the 1965 Chicago Auto Show, Chevrolet General Manager Bunkie Knudsen stifled rumors that the Chevy II would be dropped from Chevy's line-up. He knew that the second generation Chevy II, to be released in 1966, was completely restyled and would include additional performance options.

In 1966, the Chevy II received a completely restyled body that was well proportioned and looked much sleeker than the previous design. It also looked much larger than the previous model, while retaining the 110-inch wheelbase and 183-inch overall length.

Well, that's not quite true. The price is still plain as Aunt Agatha's cast iron skillet. But the rest of the Chevy II is strictly high fashion, like this Nova SS Sport Coupe's sleek roof line, its slender Strato-bucket seats. Even the super economy 100 series has such luxury touches as padded armrests and foam cushioned front seat. Wrap this around some of the many extra features available and one of the seven engines, up to 350 horsepower, and you've got quite a package. Looking for economy? You came to the right place. Looking for Jane? She ain't here.

Chevy II-Styled The Chevrolet Way

Ads for the new 1966 Nova featured a red Super Sport. Chevrolet tried to promote the Nova's image as something above a basic transportation car. The ad writers even carefully slipped in the fact that the new Nova could be purchased with a 350-horsepower engine.

Only a few styling cues were carried over to the new 1966 Chevy II. Up front was Chevy's traditional egg-crate grille and on the sides, the new Chevy II featured the same wheel opening and rocker detail as the first-generation car. The sides of the new Chevy II body were almost flat, except for a pronounced horizontal character line that ran front to rear. A slight peak to the top of the front fender rounded over to the chrome headlight bezel. The Chevy II's roofline was a semi-fastback design, but not as severe as the Chevelle and Impala rooflines. Thicker C-pillars added a more formal look to the economy car and the quarter panel had a delicate flair to the top, similar to the Impala's. The Chevy II's taillights were rectangular in shape and positioned vertically, which marked a distinct departure from Chevy's established horizontal taillight arrangement, but gave the Chevy II the appearance of a more expensive car. Front and rear bumpers were sculpted to match the shape of the car.

In 1966, the Nova Super Sport was again a distinct model offered only in the two-door sport coupe. The exterior featured thin wheelwell opening moldings that blended into the rocker panel molding. Matching the rocker molding were front and rear fender lower moldings. The full-width, ribbed, deck lid molding carried SS emblems along with the grille, and Super Sport script was placed on the rear upper edge of the quarter panel near the taillight. The Super Sport's full wheel covers had a simulated tri-bar look, since federal regulations deemed the previous style of flipper wheel cover too dangerous for pedestrians. Optional were simulated wire wheel and five-spoke mag-style wheel covers. The interior of the 1966 Super Sport Nova was well appointed, featuring the luxurious Strato bucket seats. With a four-speed or Powerglide, a special brushed chrome center console was added. The all-new instrument panel was redesigned and had the look of a scaled-down Impala panel. Added to comply to federal safety regulations was a padded instrument panel pad, padded sun visors, and glare reducing hardware.

For most designers in the automotive industry, working on a mom-and-pop transportation car like the Chevy II was not as much fun as a project like a Corvette, since the money was not available to add extras or to take the extra time to develop more exotic proposals. On the other hand, because of the limited budget and the need to make the design as efficient as possible, many of the "nuts-and-bolts" production engineers loved this type of project, because it was their job to get the car into production as quickly, easily, and inexpensively as possible. In

The 1967 Nova SS was almost identical to the 1966 model. Added to the option list were disc brakes with Rally Wheels. The numbers above the crossed flags on the front fender indicate that this 1967 Nova Super Sport is powered by a 327 engine.

the case of the 1966 Chevy II, they did their jobs exceptionally well.

In an effort to bolster Chevy's 1966 performance image, the 350-horsepower 327 was optional in the Chevy II. With this engine, the 1966 Chevy II was transformed into a true musclecar. The power-to-weight ratio was better than the SS396 Chevelle equipped with the 360-horsepower engine. When road tested, the 350-horsepower Chevy II outperformed the big block Chevelle by a large margin. *Car Life* magazine tested a Nova SS with a 350-horsepower engine for the May 1966 issue. The writers raved about the performance of the engine and balance of the chassis. "Unlike some samples from the supercar spectrum, it maintains a gentleness along with its fierce performance potential; its power/weight ratio is second to none, and it is definitely better balanced than most." Also available in the 1966 Chevy II was the 275-horsepower 327, replacing both the 250- and 300-horsepower versions of the 327.

Chevy II sales in 1966 bettered the 1965 numbers by 50,000, with a total number of units sold at 172,485. Even with its improved sales numbers, Ford's Falcon still outsold the Chevy II. Many of the extra cost options available on the Chevelle and Impala were not available on the Chevy II, no doubt because Chevrolet hoped that these extras would convince the potential buyer to move up to one of the bigger models.

In the fall of 1966, the 1967 models were delivered to the showroom. Upstaging all the models was the new Camaro. Only one notch above the Corvair in Chevy's food chain was the 1967 Chevy II, which, with the exception of a few minor trim changes, appeared identical to the 1966 model. The only major change was the addition of the disc brake option, which came standard with 14-inch, silver-painted Rally Wheels. The Super Sport model was accented in similar fashion to the 1966 model. The only obvious change was the addition of new tri-bar hubcaps. Sadly, Chevrolet dropped the 350-horsepower 327

The second-generation Nova had a much more formal design, as evidenced by the thicker C-pillar and vertical taillights. Super Sport Novas in 1967 had a minimum of chrome trim on the sides. SS models had Super Sport script on the quarter panel and a Nova SS emblem on the deck lid.

from the engine option chart, leaving the 275-horse-power 327 engine at the top of the option list. While the 275 engine was a good performer, it didn't have the savage high-revving kick of the 350.

In 1967, sales of the Chevy II slumped to a disappointing 106,500—the car's worst sales performance ever. The 1967 sales decline was probably due in large part to the release of the new Camaro, for which Chevrolet adopted a Mustang-style of marketing, by offering an inexpensive sporty car and allowing the customer to choose from a long line of options to build a car to suit. The Chevy II never offered a lengthy option list and it was probably still perceived as a car for someone in his or her golden years. But at least Chevy was not the only one having a hard time selling an economy sedan. The sales of Ford's Falcon dropped to 64,335 units in 1967. On the drawing board at General Motors was a new Chevy II that would borrow heavily from the Camaro.

Even the totally redesigned 1967 Chevy II could not escape the Chevrolet tradition of an egg-crate grille. The same pattern was carried into the background of the headlight bezel. The small bow tie in the back of the door mirror confirms that Chevy designers never missed a chance for product identification.

When the new 1968 models were introduced, the all-new Chevy II was eclipsed by the new Corvette. The Chevy II was still a mom-and-pop car that couldn't compete with the new Corvette—they were in two different leagues. Initially, because of the excitement over the Corvette, the Chevy II was ignored at the press previews. But under the new Chevy II's plain exterior was Chevrolet's simplicity and quality engineering—two factors that would make the new Chevy II a winner with journalists who drove them in road tests and with customers who bought them.

The 1968 Chevy II Nova was longer, lower, and wider than its predecessor. The wheelbase was stretched 1 inch to 111.0 inches. Only two body styles were available, a two-door sedan and a four-door sedan. The front-end sheet metal had the look of the 1967 Chevy II, with peaked fenders and large single headlamps. The grille's horizontal bars emphasized the new width. A little of the 1968 Chevelle's look

Chevy II much.

Topside, it's a neat little two-door. Underneath, it's all set to move. Beefed-up suspension, wide oval red stripes and one of the greatest V8s you've ever ordered into action. It's a 350-cu.-in. 295-hp affair with 4-barrel carburetion and 2¼" dual exhausts. Nova SS. We call it Chevy II much. You'll second the motion.

Nova SS CHEVROLET

Chevrolet aggressively advertised the new 1968 Nova SS in enthusiast magazines. Red stripe tires and hood grilles were standard with the SS option. Initially offered with only a 295-horsepower 350, the engine offerings soon included several versions of the big block.

was apparent in the thick C-pillar and semi-fastback roof, but overall, the 1968 Chevy II's design was clean and efficient and had a personality all its own.

One way to save money when manufacturing a car is to share components with other models. Doing this effectively takes a skilled engineering group. Such was the case with the 1967 Camaro and the 1968 Chevy II, where many of the chassis components were identical. The new front subframe and front suspension were shared between the two cars. The cowl—the body structure at the base of the windshield—is one of the most important components in any car. It is not only the largest structural member in a vehicle, but it also determines body height and much of the vehicle packaging. The Chevy II and the Camaro shared the same cowl. The rear suspension in both cars was also the same. The mono leaf spring was only used on the cars equipped with the base four-cylinder engine and a multi-leaf spring was fitted to all Chevy IIs with an optional engine. The change in rear springs was a result of lessons learned with the Camaro. When substantial amounts of horsepower were applied, the mono springs allowed the rear wheels to hop.

The new Chevy II had a wide range of available engines. Dropped from the list of available V-8s was the 283. Taking over as the base V-8 was the new 307-ci small block. Debuting in the Camaro in 1967, and available for the first time in a Chevy II in 1968, was the new 350-ci small block engine, rated at 295 horsepower.

The new 350 was the able replacement for the 327. It had a 4.0-inch bore, which was the same as the 327, and a 3.48-inch stroke. The small block engine that engineers 10 years earlier felt uncomfortable taking to 283 cubic inches had now grown, exceeding all expectations in durability and horsepower development. Only one 350 was available in the 1968 Chevy II, rated at 295 horsepower with 380 lb-ft of torque. This engine was standard when the Super Sport option was selected. Along with the 350 engine came heavy-duty springs, radiator, and clutch.

Also available in the 1968 Chevy II was a 325-horsepower version of the 327. This engine was the same as the 350-horsepower version installed in the Corvette. It had a long-duration hydraulic lifter cam and a Rochester Quadrajet on a cast-iron intake manifold. It came standard with the Borg Warner heavy-duty (M13) three-speed manual transmission. Optional were two Muncie four-speeds: the M20 wide-ratio and the M21 close-ratio. These three transmissions were also optional with the 295-horsepower 350, along with the two-speed Powerglide automatic transmission.

Bill "Grumpy" Jenkins ran a big block SS Nova in 1968. These cars, with their excellent power-to-weight ratio and short wheelbase, became favorites of competitors across the country. *1996, NHRA Photographic*

Chevy's engineers once again showed their foresight by making room available in the 1968 Chevy II engine compartment for the 396 big-block engine. Two 396s were available in 1968, one rated at 350 horsepower and the second at 375. Neither of these engines was shown as being available in the initial 1968 Chevy II product brochure. The Chevy II 396s were the same as those offered in the Camaro and Chevelle. The 350-horsepower version had a hydraulic cam and a Rochester Quadrajet carburetor, while the 375-horsepower version had a solid lifter cam and a large Holley four-barrel carburetor. Both 396s came standard with the same heavy-duty Borg Warner three-speed manual transmission that backed the 325-horsepower 327. Optional with the 350-horsepower version were the Muncie wide-ratio and close-ratio four-speed transmissions. The close-ratio Muncie four-speed was the optional transmission with the 375 engine, along with a heavy-duty Muncie M22 close-ratio transmission. Both the Powerglide and Turbo Hydra-Matic automatics were optional with the 350-horsepower version, but not the 375. Twelve-bolt rear axles were standard with all

high-performance engines and Positraction ratios were available from 2.73:1 to 4.88:1.

Nineteen sixty-eight also was the year that all Chevy IIs were known as Novas. Sales literature freely interchanged the names Chevy II Nova, Nova, and Chevy II from page to page. On the car, the front and rear nameplates read "Chevy II" while the quarter panel emblems read "Nova." Prior to 1968, a Nova was an optional model of the Chevy II. The Super Sport was an option in 1968, no longer a distinct model as it was in 1967. It was available on the two-door Nova Sport Coupe only. The exterior of the Super Sport featured a special hood with simulated air intakes, a black-accented grille and rear deck panel that both featured SS emblems, and Super Sport emblems on the lower edge of the front fenders. E70x14 red-line tires were standard. On the interior, the only SS identification was on the center of the deluxe steering wheel. Bucket seats (all-vinyl in black, dark blue, or gold) were not standard with the SS package, but were optional along with a gauge package and center shift console. The Nova's SS package did include the new 350-ci engine and a host

of heavy-duty chassis components and dual exhaust. Disc brakes were optional.

A "sleeper," in hot rod jargon, is a car that would go unnoticed on a street filled with traffic. It's the mundane type of car that you'd see parked in the front row at 5 P.M. at a restaurant that offers "early bird" dinner specials to senior citizens. The "sleeper of the year" is exactly what *Hot Rod* magazine called the new 1968 Chevy II Nova when the magazine tested it. *Car and Driver* echoed the same sentiments when it tested a 375-horsepower 1968 Chevy II Nova SS. "The sleeper appeals only to the most secure and sophisticated performance car fancier. There are no admiring glances from onlookers to bolster the ego. The entire driver satisfaction is based on the inward confidence that you can put the hurt on a strutting GTO or Mopar before they even realize you're a threat."

It was obvious that brains, as well as instinct, were at work in Chevrolet's Warren, Michigan, offices when the 1968 Chevy II was designed. It had the same overall look, feel, and personality as the classic 1955 Chevy. The new Chevy II offered the consumer the choice of a low-cost economy car or an inexpensive high-performance sedan. The high-performance version had performance stats that outshined a comparably equipped Chevelle SS. *Car Life* magazine was so impressed with the new Chevy II Nova that the editors named it one of their 10 best cars for 1968. "The Chevy II Nova SS presents a sensible, not terribly expensive package that comes nearer to satisfying all the people all the time than anything else we've tested this year. It's a car that's extremely eager to please, and for all around driving anywhere, it has enough personality combined with looks, handling, stamina, and economy to fit nearly any American's image of himself." The redesigned 1968 Chevy II Nova was a big hit. It outsold the 1967 version by a margin of two to one.

The musclecar era was in full swing in 1969. The insurance companies were only starting to correlate the accident rates of youthful drivers and the horsepower of the cars they were driving. It was also a time when the price of gas was low and the

octane high. Every automobile manufacturer had a musclecar on the road—even American Motors.

There were very few changes to the 1969 Chevy Nova. No longer badged or referred to as a Chevy II, it was a Nova in 1969—and all the body nameplates now said "Nova." The body styles remained the same, with the Super Sport option available on the two-door coupe. One obvious change to the exterior on the 1969 Super Sport Nova was the addition of simulated front fender louvers, which displaced the Super Sport script previously affixed to the bottom of the front fender. Also offered for the first time were the 14x7-inch sport wheels. These five-spoke simulated mag wheels were the same as those offered on the 1969 Camaro and SS396 Chevelle.

Standard with the Super Sport in 1969 were power front disc brakes and a 300-horsepower 350-ci engine, which featured the same complement of three- and four-speed manual transmissions offered in 1968. Added as an option on the 300-horsepower engine was the new Turbo Hydra-Matic 350 transmission. The trusty Powerglide was also still available on all small block offerings. The Turbo 400 was again available on the 350-horsepower 396, and a special version of that transmission could be ordered with the 375-horsepower 396.

The May 1969 issue of *Road Test* magazine featured the 1969 Nova SS powered by a 350-horsepower

In 1969, Nova Super Sports could be ordered with the 375-horsepower engine. The engine was trimmed with chrome valve covers and air cleaner lid, similar to Chevy's other SS cars. This engine was offered with a four-speed manual or a Turbo Hydra-Matic transmission.

With the new, larger body, the Nova found a whole new audience and sales improved. The 1969 models had very few changes from the previous year. One of the most noticeable was the front fender louvers on the SS models. The 1969 models were also equipped with the same sport wheels used on the SS Chevelle. This 1969 Nova Super Sport is missing its center-mounted SS grille emblem.

By 1972, the Nova Super Sport had lost much of its kick. The only engine available was a 200-horsepower 350—big blocks were no longer available. Also gone were attractive sporty wheels, replaced with a stamped-steel rim and a small hubcap. *Copyright 1978–1999 GM Corp. Used with permission of GM Media Archives*

396 backed by a Turbo Hydra-Matic transmission. The *Road Test* editors admitted in the article that they were skeptical about the big engine/light body package and were ready to find fault with the car. But the car's performance balance of topnotch acceleration with outstanding braking won them over. "It is a very workable and sporty combination. By the end of our test, we were really unhappy to give the two-door back. With many cars, we can't give them back fast enough."

In 1969, the Nova took hold of the market, selling 258,728 units. More than 7,000 of those Novas were equipped with one of the two powerful 396 engines. The performance potential of the big-block Nova was tapped into by two musclecar entrepreneurs: Don Yenko at Yenko Chevrolet in Canonsburg, Pennsylvania, and Joel Rosen, whose Motion Performance partnered with Long Island, New York's, Baldwin Chevrolet. Both of these visionaries built their own version of a take-no-prisoners 427-powered Nova SS. Today these cars are some of the most highly sought-after specialty musclecars of the era.

The 1970 Nova looked very much like, and was optioned similarly to, the 1969 models. Only minor exterior and interior trim changes were undertaken. Chevrolet continued to offer the Super Sport option, which included the 300-horsepower 350 engine along with the optional big block engines. Those big blocks marketed as 396-cubic-inch displacement had grown to 402 cubic inches, but because the 396 engine was so highly identified with performance, Chevrolet continued to market it as a 396. This was the last year Chevrolet offered the big block in the Nova.

Nineteen seventy-one was a pivotal year in the auto industry. Pressure by the insurance industry and the federal government on the auto makers to build cars that were more socially responsible took hold. All of Chevy's car lines took a hit, but the Nova was probably the most noticeable. Gone from the option list were the fire-breathing big blocks that had made their mark in the 1960s.

The 1971 Nova looked very similar to the previous year, with only minor trim changes to distinguish it from the 1970 model. A Super Sport option was available and offered a standard 350-ci four-barrel-equipped engine, but because of a lower compression ratio, it was only listed as having 270 horsepower. Released midyear was the Rally Nova. It provided the consumer with a quasi-musclecar that had the look, with stripes and Rally Wheels, but lacked the substance under the hood. The 1972 Nova Super Sport was much of the same, with a lower horsepower rating (200) due to a revised system of calculation. The super car era was coming to a close and the Nova was one of the first cars to make its exit.

In 1973, Chevrolet gave the Nova a well-deserved facelift. Most noticeable was the revised front end and quarter window treatment. Up front, the federally mandated 5-mile-per-hour front bumper took precedence. It was much larger than the previous bumper and jutted out, well ahead of the front fenders and grille. The grille was redesigned with an egg-crate pattern. Large, single headlights dominated the ends of the grille. The front edge of the front fenders was straightened up, giving the front a more formal look. Keeping with the formal look, the rear edge of the C-pillar was more vertical. In the rear, the bumper was enlarged to meet the 1973 rear impact requirements of 2 1/2 miles per hour. A Super Sport option that included a large body side stripe, blacked-out grille, heavy-duty suspension, and 14x6 Rally Wheels was available. Any engine from a small list of selections could be specified for the Super Sport, but the best engine offering was a 350-ci engine rated at 175 horsepower. The Nova SS returned for 1974 with little change, though the Powerglide transmission and the 307-ci V-8 were missing from the option list.

In 1975, Chevrolet completely redesigned the Nova. It was a stylish car and offered the SS option in the two-door coupe model. Cars with big engines that accelerated well were now a social and financial burden. By this time in history, a performance car was thought of as one with good brakes and good gas mileage. Big block musclecars that were just five years old were selling for pennies on the dollar. In 1976, Chevrolet offered its last Nova SS. And so, after 13 years, Chevy's simple transportation car had reverted to its roots.

Chevy RPO Listings

In 1963, Chevrolet changed the way it coded its options. Previously, options were given a random number. For instance, prior to 1963, an optional Powerglide transmission was 313 and tinted glass was 398. In 1963, all sales identification codes were revised by placing them into groupings. Now each code would contain a letter prefix that would indicate a Universal Parts Classification (UPC), followed by a two-digit number that would indicate the individual option. The UPC letter codes went from A to Z and the option codes from 01 to 99. Transmissions were now coded from M01 to M99 and engines from K01 to L99. When reference is made to an M20 four-speed, it's simply the option code for that particular transmission. The same is true for engine codes, like L34 or L79. Paint and trim codes retained a three digit number. The catchall option code has a Z prefix. The Z-code options are also those in which there is a combination of significant body, chassis, engine, and interior items. These options are best exemplified by special, low-production cars such as the Z28 Camaro or the Z11-optioned 1963 Impala. Z11 was also the code given to the Camaro pace cars. This chart contains the basic RPO codes.

RPO Code	UPC Group
A01-D99	Body
F01-F39	Frame
F50-F99	Front suspension
G50-H99	Rear axle and suspension
J50-J99	Brakes
K01-L99	Engine
M01-M99	Transmission
N01-N29	Fuel & Exhaust
N30-N49	Steering
P01-S99	Wheels & Tires
T50-T59	Sheet Metal
T60-U99	Electrical & Instruments
V01-V29	Radiator & Grille
V30-V99	Bumpers & Miscellaneous
Z01-Z49	Chevrolet Special items

The 1970 Chevelle SS lacked exterior frills. Other than thin bright moldings outlining the wheel openings and windows, there was no extra body chrome. Hood and deck lid stripes were optional, but they became standard (along with racing-style hood pins) when the cowl induction hood was ordered. The wheels on the 1970 Chevelle SS were the same 14x7 inchers that were on the 1969 SS models.

Chapter 4

Chevelle SS
A Little Bigger, A Lot Faster

In the early 1960s' battle of small cars, Chevrolet's Chevy II, which was designed to compete with Ford's Falcon, was losing ground. Ford also took the offensive in 1963 and released the midsized Fairlane. To match car lines with Ford, Chevrolet introduced the Chevelle in 1964. This was Chevy's third new vehicle in four years. The 1964 Chevelle was based on the "A-body" design from Fisher Body, which was shared by the Pontiac Tempest, Olds F-85, and Buick Skylark. One distinguishing styling feature of these cars was the use of curved side glass. There are no straight lines in a car body and curved side glass gave the stylists more freedom and creativity in their designs. Each division's offering was highly distinctive, even though they all shared the same basic platform.

The 1964 Chevelle was an efficiently packaged car. It fit perfectly between the too-small Chevy II and the too-big full-size Chevrolet. On the inside the Chevelle was almost as roomy as a full-size Chevy while the exterior was a full 16 inches shorter. The 1964 Chevelle, because of its size, simplicity, and performance, was often compared to the 1955 Chevy. Both were attractive, affordable, and sold well.

General Motors had a styling philosophy for the design of all its cars. Whatever the make or model, it must be identifiable—highly identifiable—when driving toward or away from you. Chevrolet accomplished this objective with the Chevelle. Another goal was to carry consistent styling cues across all models in the car line. The new Chevelle had the look of a scaled-down full-size Chevy, but it also had its own character. The egg-crate oval-shaped grille brought a strong image of the full-size Chevy, but the sculpted sides and unique oval-shaped rear treatment were distinctly Chevelle. It was difficult to find fault with the look of the 1964 Chevelle.

Eleven 1964 Chevelle models were offered in three series: a base 300, a Malibu, and a Super Sport. The Super Sport was a distinct model available as either a two-door sport coupe or a convertible. Each of the models was offered with either a basic six or V-8 engine. In addition, the El Camino returned after a three year absence. Built on a Chevelle platform, it was Chevy's reply to the popular Ford Ranchero.

Styling trends have their ups and downs. In the mid-1950s, cars were lavished with lots of chrome. The late-1950s saw the tail fins rise and fall. When Bill Mitchell took over as the head of styling, he began deleting chrome and shrinking tail fins. His staff of designers trimmed the 1964 Super Sport Chevelle in a minimalist style. The only bright exterior trim outlined the car's side with a thin strip that started at the front fender and ran the length of the car along the belt line and terminated at the taillight. Thin moldings also framed the wheel opening edges and rocker panels. This minimal amount of exterior chrome spoke highly of the Chevelle's exceptional styling. The Super Sport's wheel covers were borrowed from the 1964 Impala Super Sport. They were dished with a tri-bar spinner. The fine features of these wheel covers complemented the 1964 Chevelle Super Sport's overall look.

The interior of the 1964 Chevelle Super Sport was as attractive and classy as the exterior. The Super Sport had a unique instrument cluster that included

When the 1964 Chevelle was introduced, the Super Sport was one of the most popular models. For an additional $162 over the standard Malibu, the Super Sport customer received bucket seats, SS body trim, and full wheel covers identical to the ones on the Impala SS. A close inspection of the SS emblem and script on the quarter panel reveals that this preproduction model was named "Nova SS." *Copyright 1978–1999 GM Corp. Used with permission of GM Media Archives*

gauges instead of idiot lights. Super Sport identification was located above the glove box door and on the door panels. A console was included on the SS models equipped with the floor-shifted four-speed manual or Powerglide transmission, but the standard three-speed transmission was column-shifted and no console was installed. Bucket seats were standard on the Super Sport.

A variety of Chevy's six-cylinder and V-8 engines were available on the 1964 Super Sport Chevelle. The 194-ci 120-horsepower six was the standard engine, and a 155-horsepower 230-ci six was optional. Transmissions for these engines included the basic three-speed manual, overdrive, and Powerglide.

The base V-8 for the 1964 Chevelle was the 195-horsepower, 283-ci small block. A 220-horsepower version was optional for $53.80 and featured a four-barrel carburetor and dual exhaust. The 220-horsepower 283 small block V-8 first saw duty in 1957

and had been an excellent workhorse ever since. Both 283s came standard with a three-speed manual transmission, but a four-speed manual and Powerglide were optional. The two-barrel-equipped 195-horsepower engine could also be ordered with a three-speed overdrive transmission.

The 1964 Chevelle Salisbury rear axle design was similar to those used on the 10-series Chevy trucks. It was much stronger than the standard passenger car rear axle and could be identified by its 10-bolt cover. It was available in a wide range of ratios that were matched to specific engine, transmission, and option combinations. Positraction was a $37.70 option.

Chevrolet used a body-on-frame construction for the new Chevelle. The X-frame design used on the full-size cars since 1958 was abandoned for an all-new perimeter frame. Four different frames of the same basic design were used for the 1964 Chevelle. One frame was used for coupes and sedans and one of equal length with two additional body

Chevrolet made the SS option available in both the sport coupe and convertible. From the first day of production, two versions of the reliable 283-ci engines were available. Later in the production year, the 327 engine could be ordered. The small "V" on the front fender indicates that this vehicle is powered by a 283. Copyright 1978–1999 GM Corp. Used with permission of GM Media Archives

mounts was used on the convertible. Station wagon and El Camino frames were 3.25 inches longer than the others. Side rails were an open C section, except on the convertible and El Camino, where they were closed for extra rigidity. Spanning the frame were three welded cross-members. The front cross-member, which was the largest and was fully boxed, supported the engine and front suspension. A large deep channel-section cross-member above the rear axle provided mounts for the coil spring pockets, shock absorber mounts, and upper control arms. A smaller, open-section rail tied the rear of the frame together. One removable cross-member was used as a rear transmission support. The frame served as the pattern for the next generation full-size Chevy, released in 1965.

The 1964 Chevelles sold well. It was the right size and had a good mix of options to suit any taste. But performance enthusiasts were disappointed in the selection of engines available. Chevrolet General Manager Bunkie Knudsen had been out-foxed by his protégé at Pontiac, John DeLorean, who released

the hot GTO in 1964, but Knudsen would get his revenge in 1965.

For 1965, the Chevelle received a minor facelift that rounded and softened the lines of the 1964 Chevelle body. This restyling also made the car look longer and lower. The front fenders, hood, and grille were new. Larger taillights were installed and the back-up lights were relocated to the rear bumper.

The 1965 Chevelle Super Sport models were also devoid of the side molding that was standard on the Malibu. The exterior of the Super Sport was identified by SS emblems on the quarter panels and deck lid. The grille and rear taillight panel were accented in black. Added were chrome rocker panel moldings and special full wheel covers with an SS logo in the center. The interior was fitted with bucket seats and a console on cars equipped with a Powerglide and four-speed. A small SS emblem was added to the glove box door.

Chevelle's performance image had not been established in 1964. The 1964 GTO staked out a lot of what had traditionally been Chevrolet's exclusive

In 1965, Chevy made only small changes to the front and rear of the Chevelle. An SS package was again offered in both the sport coupes and convertibles. In front of the rear wheel opening on this preproduction model are two small moldings that never made it onto the production models. *Copyright 1978–1999 GM Corp. Used with permission of GM Media Archives*

performance territory. In an attempt to save face in 1964, Chevy installed the 250- and 300-horsepower 327s as a midyear addition, which helped, but fell short of the mark the GTO set with its 325-horsepower base engine or 348-horsepower optional engine. In 1965, Chevrolet's best production line effort to counter the GTO was the addition of the L79, 350-horsepower 327 engine, which was mechanically identical to the Corvette's 350-horsepower engine. It was available on all Chevelle models and came standard with a three-speed manual transmission, or optional four-speed manual. This engine was a big improvement, but it lacked the torque of the GTO's 389-ci engine. The new Chevelle, even in Super Sport trim, also lacked the panache of the smartly styled 1965 GTO.

On February 15, 1965, Bunkie Kundsen got his revenge with the limited release of the Z-16 Chevelle. The Z-16 was a fully optioned Chevelle Super Sport with a special high-performance version of the new 396 engine. Chevrolet started with the 425-

horsepower engine and replaced the cam with a slightly tamer hydraulic lifter version. This dropped the horsepower to 375. This engine was backed up with a four-speed transmission and every heavy-duty option on the Chevelle's lengthy list. Also included were a tilt wheel, stereo radio, vinyl top, Firestone gold-line tires, and simulated mag wheel hubcaps. Special SS396 emblems were added to the deck lid and the right side of the instrument panel. Chevrolet finally had its super car!

Only 201 of these special SSs were built, 200 coupes and one convertible. Chevrolet's PR group looked back to the success they had had in 1961 when the Impala Super Sport was released and they set out to make sure every automotive journalist who wanted to drive a Z-16 had the opportunity. A few Z-16s were also given to high-profile television personalities, other selected VIPs, and Chevrolet executives.

There were never any product brochures or print ads for the Z-16 Chevelle; instead, the car

On the 1965 Chevelle SS, Chevy designers removed the body side molding that had been standard on the Malibu. SS emblems were added to the quarter panels and deck lid. Chrome rocker panel moldings were added, along with special full wheel covers with an SS logo in the center. Optional were simulated mag wheel covers.

made a name for itself with its performance and image. With the Z-16, Chevrolet proved it could build cars that created excitement in the performance-hungry automotive community. The anticipation for a 396-powered Chevelle for 1966 was high and Chevrolet wasn't about to disappoint anyone. Chevelle, like all other Chevrolet products except the Corvair, set sales records in 1965 and soundly outsold its major competition, the Ford Fairlane. And, to add an exclamation point to the sales statistics, over 81,000 of the Chevelle's sales in 1965 were Super Sport models.

The 1966 Chevelle was completely restyled and featured a fastback roofline on the two-door sport coupes. Overall, the design of the 1966 Chevelle now resembled a scaled-down full-size Chevy. Similar to the full-size Chevy, the tops of the quarter panels had a slight flare. At the end of the quarter panel was an end cap that housed a recessed taillight. The leading edge of the front fenders was cut back, giving the front end of the new Chevelle the same forward lean as the 1966 Impala. From the side, the Chevelle Sport Coupe had the same fastback roofline as the Impala, except the Chevelle's rear window was countersunk, creating two distinctive sail panels.

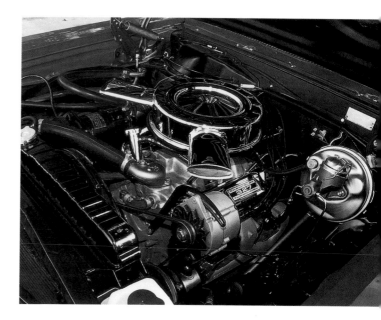

In 1965, Chevy upped the performance ante of the Chevelle by offering the 350-horsepower L-79 327-ci engine. This high-revving engine gave the Chevelle GTO-like performance at bargain basement prices. But even in SS trim, the Chevelle couldn't match the image of the GTO.

67

The Z-16's engine was a slightly detuned version of the Corvette's 425-horsepower engine. Rated at 375, it retained all the Corvette's heavy-duty components, except the solid lifter camshaft, which was replaced with a long-duration hydraulic cam. *Mike Mueller*

Now that you mention it, yes, it does look lean and hungry.

This is an SS 396, a Chevelle that's swallowed a snootful of Turbo-Jet V8—396 cubic inches of it—with ratings of 325, 360 or 375 horsepower. The 325 rating is standard; the other two you have to specify because they cost extra. But it bears mentioning at this point that the 375-horsepower job endows the SS 396 with a power-to-weight ratio of 9.4 to 1. And that, performance fans, is hardly what you'd call unimpressive.

Of special interest, too, is the fact that every SS 396 swings right from the factory with stiffer springs and shocks, a bigger front stabilizer bar, special frame reinforcements and a set of red stripe tires on wide-base wheels.

Know what? You're beginning to look a bit lean and hungry yourself. Do drive an SS 396 at your Chevrolet dealer's.

Performance The Chevrolet Way

In 1966, Chevelle was back in the musclecar parade with the new SS396. Ads like this one touted the SS396's power and standard heavy-duty equipment.

In 1966, a Super Sport Chevelle no longer meant bucket seats and any engine—it meant a powerful engine, tons of image, and a lengthy option list. In 1966, the Super Sport was transformed into SS396, with the addition of two versions of Chevy's hot 396-ci big-block engine. The 396 made a strong debut in 1965, and proved itself to be anvil-tough and loaded with horsepower potential. The SS396 was available in three horsepower ratings starting at 325, a midrange engine at 360, and a take-no-prisoners 375-horsepower version. The SS396 exterior was understated, with minimal ornamentation. In 1966, the battle for musclecar superiority among the manufacturers was like gangs of toughs fighting it out with knives and chains in a phone booth. In 1966, the SS396 Chevelle came out without a scratch.

The 1965 Z-16 Chevelle suffered from the same over-optioned-and-too-expensive affliction as the original 1961 Impala Super Sport. To lighten the consumer's burden, the 1966 SS396 was stripped to the bare bones. The basic SS396 Chevelle was available in either a two-door hardtop at a base price of $2,776 or as a convertible for $2,962. The base engine was the 325-horsepower 396, which was identical to the one installed in the full-size Chevy. A Borg Warner fully synchronized three-speed manual transmission with a floor-mounted shifter was standard. A heavy-duty 12-bolt differential was also standard, but Positraction was not. Heavy-duty front and rear springs and shocks were also standard, along with 6-inch-wide steel wheel rims mounting 7.75x14 red-line tires. Early production cars were fitted with small, dog-dish hubcaps, and full wheel covers were optional. A midyear change dropped the small hubcap and the full wheel cover became standard. Mag-styled full wheel covers that debuted in 1965 were optional.

The exterior of the SS396 Chevelle was low key. Super Sport chrome script dressed the quarter panels.

70

Mounted on the front fender were the unique 396 flags. Small SS396 badges were located in the center of the blacked-out grille and on the rear panel between the taillights. Almost every midsize muscle-car in 1966 had some type of hood vent or scoop, and the SS396 followed form. The two side-facing hood vents were the most distinctive exterior features on the new SS396. While the vents conformed to the trend of the day, the Chevelle's hood looked awkward when compared to the GTO's smoothly styled scoop.

The interior of the SS396 Chevelle was Spartan. A bench seat was standard, available only in solid color vinyl trim. Basic instrumentation on the SS396 was minimal; even the tach was an option. To Chevrolet's credit, the option list for the SS396 Chevelle was robust, which the average buyer took advantage of to add the extras necessary to suit his or her needs. Most buyers thought in terms of horsepower, and the optional 360-horsepower engine cost only an additional $150. The 360-horse-power engine was similar to the 325-horsepower engine with the exception of a longer-duration hydraulic lifter cam and a large Holley four-barrel carburetor on an aluminum intake manifold. A 375-horsepower engine was on the option list for an additional $235, but this engine was not for the faint-hearted. The 375-horse engine was similar to the Z-16's, except in 1966, it was equipped with a long-duration mechanical lifter cam. Most SS396s were

Chevrolet completely redesigned the 1966 Chevelle. The front had the same forward lean as the full-size models. SS396 models featured Super Sport script on the quarter panels, an SS396 emblem in the blacked-out grille and on the rear deck, and a special hood with side-facing simulated vents. (The Rally Wheels on this car were not available until 1967.)

Early-production 1966 SS396 Chevelles were fitted with small dog-dish–style hubcaps. Later in the year, full wheel covers became standard. All 1966 models were equipped with red stripe tires. *Copyright 1978–1999 GM Corp. Used with permission of GM Media Archives*

delivered with a Muncie four-speed manual transmission, which was available with either wide- or close-ratio gearing. Available as an option on the 325- and 360-horsepower engines was Chevrolet's two-speed Powerglide.

Most buyers selected the optional Strato bucket seats, which were leaner and had a more appealing look than the previous, beefy bucket seat design of Corvair Monza heritage. A chrome center console was available to those ordering bucket seats. Rounding out the interior were instrumentation packages, a tilt wheel, a woodgrained steering wheel, and an AM/FM radio.

Chevrolet loaned *Hot Rod* magazine's Eric Dahlquist a new, four-speed, 360-horsepower 1966 SS396. In the February 1966 issue he wrote: "As a synopsis of the random reflections that ran through our mind as we returned the car to the Chevrolet zone office, it could be said this SS396 was the type of vehicle we hated to part with. It has just the right measures of ride, handling and acceleration that would make it the nuts for all kinds of long trips. It's a fun car for today's dull traffic, and if it helps relieve tedium of travel, you can't ask much more." The new SS396 Chevelle also received favorable reviews as the *Hot Rod* staff drove it around Los Angeles. "All the time we drove the SS396, it drew a great

To keep the base price down on the 1966 SS396, many of the extras included on other musclecars of the era were optional. Bucket seats, four-speed transmissions, and center consoles were among the most popular options. The simulated woodgrain sport steering wheel was also an option.

In 1967, Chevy gave the Chevelle a mild facelift. The SS396 models also received a new hood featuring shapely twin blisters fitted with chrome grilles. Disc brakes were available as an option and required Chevy's new Rally Wheels.

In 1967, the Chevelle SS396 came standard with a 325-horsepower engine. Optional engines were rated at 350 (down 10 horsepower from 1966) and 375 horsepower. All SS396 engines were accentuated with chrome rocker covers and air cleaners.

deal of attention from the younger set who seemed to dig everything about it."

Chevy's long-vacant performance sedan niche was filled with the SS396. It quickly reestablished Chevrolet's performance image, and by year's end 72,272 SS396 models had been sold in 1966. Its perfect combination of size, power, image, and low cost was responsible for taking sales away from both Nova SS and Impala SS models. But for the same reason, the SS396 was also responsible for stealing sales away from all the other manufacturers.

Buick (with its GS) and Olds (with its 442) were convincing everyone that in addition to building large luxurious cars, they could also build some serious muscle. Ford jumped on the musclecar bandwagon with its big block-powered Fairlane and Mercury Cyclone. Offered in limited supply was a 427-ci, 425-horsepower version. Those cars, along with Chrysler's Street Hemi, provided stiff competition on the street, strip, and showroom for the SS396. These other cars were also expensive and in some cases, limited in availability. The 1967 SS396 was a reasonably priced performance car and it could be found as close as the nearest Chevy dealer. The base two-door hardtop listed for $2,825, while a buyer could upgrade to the 350-horsepower engine for only $105.35 or go for the ultimate thrill ride with the 375-horsepower engine for an additional $237. A four-speed transmission cost only $105.35 and Positraction added $42.15. Disc brakes were available for the first time on a Chevelle for only $79, which included Rally Wheels. Also available for the first time on either the 325- or 350-horsepower engine was the Turbo Hydra-Matic 400 transmission. At $147, it was a few dollars more than the Powerglide, but worth every penny. It was hard to pass up a musclecar that cost so little, but offered so much, which is probably why Chevrolet sold 62,785 SS396 Chevelles that year.

In 1968, an entirely new Chevelle with a dramatic fastback look was introduced. The new Chevelle was styled with a long hood and short deck that was similar to the new 1968 Nova. The tread was 1 inch wider and the wheelbase was 3 inches shorter than its 1967 predecessor, yet the new Chevelle looked longer due to its semi-fastback roof styling and long hood. Hidden wipers were standard on all Chevelle models, except for the base 300 series. Chevy designers extended the rear edge of the hood over the cowl to hide the wipers. It was a simple piece of engineering that tucked away the unsightly wipers and gave the front end a cleaner look.

All of the new 1968 cars were required to meet a new set of federally mandated safety standards, most of which focused on changes to a vehicle's interior. Front seat shoulder harnesses, previously optional, were now required, but, unfortunately, most

The 1967 Chevelle received a mild facelift. The basic body was the same, but Chevrolet added new front fenders, hood, and rear treatment. The new body components gave the appearance of a slightly heavier car. The front fenders had the same aggressive forward lean as the 1966 Chevelle. The grille area was opened slightly, but no longer wrapped around the edge of the fender. The larger, egg-crate-pattern grille featured wider horizontal bars, which gave the front an appearance of width. New end caps were fitted to the quarter panels and a new larger taillight design wrapped around to the side. It was a fitting upgrade to the 1966 model.

The Chevelle SS396 chassis and engine combinations were the same as in 1966, except for the optional L34 engine, which now rated 350 horsepower instead of 360. Motor Trend magazine tested three 1967 SS396 Chevelles. The hot 375-horsepower version turned in some impressive times. Its quarter-mile elapsed time was 14.9 seconds at 96 miles per hour. From zero to 60 the SS396 tripped the clocks in 6.5 seconds. All of the tests were run in full street trim with the standard F70-14 wide oval tires. Along with the engine's performance, the reviewers were ecstatic about the Chevelle's suspension. Motor Trend magazine's Robert Shilling wrote, "The SS396 is far and away the best handling and riding GM product we've driven in a long time."

In 1967 the SS396 had some stiff competition from Chevrolet's sister divisions and other manufacturers. The GTO had a loyal following and both

In 1967, the performance enthusiast had a wide selection of cars from which to chose. In addition to the competition from Ford and Chrysler, Chevy's sister divisions (with the exception of Cadillac), were all producing their own musclecars. Once in the Chevrolet dealer showroom, a customer looking for an SS396 Chevelle could have easily been drawn to the new Camaro. Even with all these distractions, there were 63,006 SS396 Chevelles sold. *Copyright 1978–1999 GM Corp. Used with permission of GM Media Archives*

consumers found using them difficult and left the belts clipped to the headliner. To reduce side impact injury, the door armrests were redesigned, and now featured a softer material and a deeper, thicker design that shielded the occupant from the interior door handles.

Everything on the inside of the cars was scrutinized. Even the glove box door lock was redesigned for passenger safety. The new door latch required a twist of the knob to open the door. The previous design allowed the door to open during an accident, creating an additional hazard to passengers. All reflective surfaces were changed to prevent driver distractions from glare, which meant bright chrome was changed to a textured, dull chrome or painted surface. Window regulator handles, door lock knobs, and ash trays were redesigned to yield under a prescribed force. In addition to a padded instrument panel (a federal requirement beginning in 1966), vinyl-coated foam padding was added to all windshield A-pillars. Dome lamps were now made

of plastic with no sharp corners. Interior designers now accepted an expanded job description that included human safety engineering.

Under the hood, changes were made to all 1968 models to meet new exhaust emission requirements. Engineers found that higher engine temperatures reduced hydrocarbon emissions, so all Chevy engines were equipped with a 195-degree thermostat. Two different systems were used by Chevrolet to control exhaust emission: the Controlled Combustion System (CCS) or the air injection reactor system (AIR). The AIR system was similar to the one introduced in 1966 on Chevys with California emissions equipment. In 1968, the AIR system was used on all models equipped with manual transmissions. The CCS increased combustion efficiency through specific carburetor and timing calibrations and also included thermostatically controlled closed-element air cleaners.

Lower hood profiles and increased engine temperatures in 1968 meant an expansion in the use of

75

more efficient cross-flow radiators. Traditional carburetor-to-accelerator pedal rod and pivot linkage gave way to a new cable-controlled system on the Chevelle. This new design—also used on the Camaro and Chevy II with the L-6 engine—gave engineers a great deal of flexibility with engine compartment packaging.

The 1968 Chevelle was available in four different series: the base Chevelle 300, the upgraded Malibu, the Concours wagon, and the SS396. Super Sport Chevelles were classified as distinct models for 1968, and they came in two sporty forms: a two-door hardtop and a convertible. Blacked-out trim was applied abundantly to the SS396 models. The grille was almost entirely black, as was the panel between the taillights. On lighter-colored cars, the rocker panels were painted black, while darker cars featured body-color rockers. The SS396 models had contrasting body stripes that wrapped over the hood and down the side just above the rockers. The SS396 had a twin dome hood with nonfunctional chrome grilles in the rear. Distinctive SS396 badges were placed in the center of the grille and rear deck. All 1968 models were required to have side marker lights, and Chevy designers neatly married the front ones with a 396 emblem. The taillights wrapped around the end cap to provide a rear side marker light—a clever attention to detail that resulted in a clean overall look.

The engine line-up for 1968 was the same as in 1967 with a base 325-horsepower engine, a hotter 350-horsepower optional engine, and the steamy-hot L78 375-horsepower engine. Disc brakes with Rally Wheels were an option, but the standard drum brakes were improved with the addition of finned front drums.

The 1968 Chevelle was an outstanding car that was almost overlooked in the excitement created by the new Corvette. More than 400,000 Chevelles were sold in 1968—62,785 of which were SS396 models. The SS gave the performance buyer a wide range of

In 1968, Chevy completely redesigned the Chevelle, giving it a larger and more rounded appearance. The SS396 Chevelle was now a distinct model for 1968, instead of an option to the Chevelle. Blacked-out trim was used extensively on the SS396 models. On all SS396s, the grille was almost entirely black and, on lighter-colored cars, the rocker panels were painted black. Contrasting body stripes, which wrapped over the hood and down the sides, were added.

In 1968, the Chevelle sport coupes received a new fastback roofline. On the SS396 models, red-line tires were standard along with full wheel covers. Chevy's wide range of luxury or performance options allowed the SS396 customer to build the boulevard cruiser or race car of his or her choice. *Copyright 1978–1999 GM Corp. Used with permission of GM Media Archives*

options with a new dash of style. The 396-ci engine was in its fourth year of production and was on its way to becoming a legend. By 1968, SS396 had become an icon for the term "musclecar."

In 1969, Chevrolet carried over a majority of the 1968 Chevelle. Vent windows were deleted on all sport coupe and convertible models in favor of a one-piece side-glass and Astro Ventilation. On the exterior, a new grille and rear quarter end caps were the extent of the changes. Because of the new end caps, rear side marker lights were added to the quarter panels. New 14x7-inch, Magnum-styled steel wheels that featured a slender five-spoke design and bright trim ring were the standard wheels on the SS396. Power front disc brakes were included with the SS396. The SS396 was no longer a separate model, but rather a $347.60 option in 1969 that could be added to the Malibu coupe, convertible, or the two-door post sedan 300 Deluxe model. This made 1969 the only year the SS option could be added to a body other than a two-door sport coupe or convert-

ible. Two different body stripes were available in 1969, a slender full-length side stripe or Band-Aid–style stripes that would become available at the end of the model year.

The engine line-up was again the same as previous years, with one exception: The L72 427-ci engine was available in limited supplies through Chevrolet's COPO (Central Office Production Order) backdoor. The L72 427 was a 425-horsepower Corvette engine that could only be ordered with a four-speed manual or Turbo Hydra-Matic transmission. It should also be noted that late in the 1969 model year, the 396 engine was overbored to 402 cubic inches, but the engines continued to be called by the 396 designation that everyone was so familiar with. RPO L89, which was available for a fat $647.75, added aluminum heads to an L78 375-horsepower 396. With the addition of the COPO 427 and L89 aluminum heads, Chevy added enough power to the Chevelle to make a Street Hemi owner cower with fear. And, just when Chevy fans thought things

Chevy made only minor changes to the 1969 Chevelle. Vent windows were deleted, giving the car a cleaner overall look. The 1968's SS396 wrap-over body stripes were revised to a single body side stripe that could be deleted. The most noticeable change to the 1969 model was the new 14x7-inch Magnum-styled steel wheels that featured a slender five-spoke design and bright trim ring.

couldn't get any better, the 1970 Super Sport Chevelles were released.

Musclecar historians look back to 1970 as the final big battle of the war. In the fall of 1969, every manufacturer locked and loaded its biggest guns for another year of the horsepower wars. In addition to Mopar's Hemi cars, they had the 440 engine equipped with three Holley two-barrel carburetors in a wide variety of bodies. Over at Ford, the Cobra Jet engine was a proven performer and they were saber rattling with their massive Boss 429. The smell of high octane was in the air and every motor head was getting high on it.

The late-year infusion of extra horsepower to the SS396 in 1969 proved that Chevrolet wasn't about to yield any more territory. For the 1970 model year, Chevy rolled out a completely new Super Sport model that wowed everyone. It was completely restyled, inside and out, and offered more power than ever before.

The 1970 Chevelle rolled on the same 112-inch wheel base frame as the 1969 model. The all-new body no longer looked like a scaled-down Impala, but it did carry a few of the larger car's styling cues, the most dramatic of which were the subtle blisters that were added to the surfaces around the front and rear wheel openings. "We thought the sides should have more interest or detailing," says Chevrolet designer Dave Holls. "I was very interested in European rally cars that started not to have wheel lips, but the surface around the wheel opening faired out. The best execution of this design came about on the '70 Chevelle Super Sport with its bigger tires." This concept was first seen on the 1969 Impala, but not with such a dramatic result as on the Chevelle. The Chevelle coupe's rear window had a very pronounced concave shape that was similar to the Impala Custom Coupe and Caprice. The front end was a more formal design with the quad headlights separated from the grille. The grille was rec-

El Camino SS

In 1959, Chevrolet introduced the El Camino. It had the styling of a full-size Chevrolet with the utility of a small pickup truck. The idea was not new; prior to World War II several manufacturers had tinkered with car/truck hybrids. In 1957, Ford Motor Company introduced the successful car/truck mix with its Ranchero. For two years, Ford had the, albeit small, market to itself. Not wanting to miss any market segment, Chevrolet countered in 1959 with the El Camino. Like the Ranchero, it was built on a full-size platform. In 1960, Ford downsized its Ranchero onto the Falcon platform. The Corvair Step Side provided Chevy a somewhat equivalent model. In 1961, Chevrolet dropped the El Camino, but it was reinstated in 1964 with the introduction of the Chevelle. The new El Camino had all the good looks of a Chevelle and more load-carrying capacity than the Falcon-based Ranchero.

In 1967, El Camino owners finally had the option of ordering a big block engine. It was the only Chevelle model in which a big block could be specified without ordering an SS396 coupe or convertible. Conversely, it was the only big block Chevelle without Super Sport trim. In 1968, that changed; a 396 Super Sport version of the El Camino could be ordered. It had all the bells and whistles of the regular SS396 and, in addition, it had a pickup bed. In 1970 an SS396 and SS454 version of the El Camino were offered. It was at that time that the insurance and government buzzards were circling, looking to pick the last bits of meat off of the musclecar carcass. But unlike the death of the SS coupes and convertibles, the El Camino SS continued well into the 1980s, but only as a trim package without a high-performance engine.

The El Camino was not left out when the musclecar era reached its peak in 1970. Offered with both the SS396 and SS454 packages, the El Camino offered the advantage of a small pickup, the comfort of a sedan, and the tire-smoking performance of the hottest musclecar.

In 1969, Chevy changed the SS396 from a distinct model to an option. The SS396 option could be added to the convertible, sport coupe (pictured), or, for the first time, the 300 Deluxe model coupe, which was a two-door post sedan. Included with the option were standard front disc brakes. *Dale Amy*

tangular in shape and had a slight V shape in the plan view. Flowing back from the grille was the raised center of the hood. The Super Sport models had a special hood with a raised rectangular dome over the engine. The rear featured a wide rear bumper with large rectangular inset taillights. Below the rear bumper was a small valence panel that was painted body color.

In 1970, Chevrolet continued the Super Sport as an option on the Chevelle. There were actually two Super Sport options: the Z-25 for the SS396, and the Z15 for the SS454. These options were only available on two-door sport coupes and convertibles. On the exterior, both versions were virtually identical, except for the engine designation below the SS emblems on the front fenders.

The Super Sport Chevelle in 1970 was devoid of any body side moldings. The only chrome was a small molding around the wheel openings. With the exception of the center SS emblem and two thin moldings separated by a slender body-color bar, the

grille was entirely blacked out. Between the taillights there was a blacked-out panel with an SS emblem on the right side. On the side of each front fender there was an SS emblem with either a 396 or 454, depending on the engine installed. These engine designations were just small enough that someone had to look closely to decipher them. All Chevelle SSs were equipped with the same SS wheels that were introduced in 1969. These wheels were fitted with F70x14 white letter, white stripe, or red-line tires. Body stripes were optional, but became standard when the cowl induction hood was ordered. The cowl induction hood had a vacuum-actuated door at the rear which opened when the throttle was wide open. This allowed cool outside air to be drawn into the carburetor. The cowl induction also included racing-style hood pins.

The interior of the 1970 Chevelle was also completely restyled. In front of the driver, the new instrument panel had three large circular dials on a black panel. A bench seat was standard, trimmed in

81

For the 1970 model year, Chevy rolled out a completely new Chevelle that had a look all its own. One of the most dramatic body elements were the subtle blisters added to the surfaces around the wheel openings. These fender forms looked especially good with the fat F70x14 white letter tires. The well-balanced front end featured quad headlights and, on the SS, a blacked-out grille.

cloth and vinyl for the sport coupes and all vinyl in convertibles. If bucket seats were specified, they were trimmed in vinyl. The upper forward portion of each door panel featured a small SS emblem, as did the center of the steering wheel.

In 1970, selecting an engine for a Chevelle Super Sport model was serious business. Deleted from the list was the 325-horsepower 396. For 1970, the base 396 (which actually displaced 402 cubic inches) was the 350-horsepower version. There were two optional 375-horsepower 396 engines: the L78 and the aluminum-headed L89. When buyers specified an SS454, their base engine was rated at 360 horsepower and featured a 10.25:1 compression ratio, a Rochester Quadrajet four-barrel carburetor, and a long-duration hydraulic lifter cam. The LS6 454 was rated at 450 horsepower. Its compression ratio was 11.25:1 and it offered a long-duration solid lifter cam. Both 454s had a whopping 500 lb-ft of torque.

There were only two basic transmission selections: a Turbo Hydra-Matic 400 or a four-speed manual. Three-speed transmissions were not available on any SS Chevelle in 1970. The M-20 was the standard wide-ratio four-speed on the SS396 and the M-21 close-ratio was standard on the SS454 and optional on the SS396. Optional was the heavy-duty M-22 four-speed. All of these transmissions were shifted by Muncie linkage. The only rear axle gear ratio available from the factory was 3.31:1, though a dealer-installed 4.10 was available. A wide range of rear gear sets from 2.73 to 4.88:1 could be ordered at any Chevrolet dealership parts department.

Back in 1970, and even now, no self-respecting journalist would pass up the chance to thrash one of these beasts—especially an LS6 SS454 with a four-speed transmission. This was the opportunity *Hot Rod* magazine's Steve Kelly had for the February 1970 edition. On the drag strip, running in street trim, the SS454 turned 13.44 seconds at 108 miles per hour. The biggest problem was trying to get the Firestone F70-14 tires to hook up. "Any throttle stabbing off the line would cause the tires to go up in smoke, and the car generally wanted to get sideways as a result." Kelly went on to say how comfortable the car was to drive in traffic and how well it handled, but that it was thirsty, gulping premium fuel at a rate of 8.4 miles per gallon. "There were a lot more things we liked about this car than we found not to our liking. It's obvious the SS Malibu 454/450 isn't meant for paper routes or drivers who don't like being able to go quick and corner flat. An expensive proposition is what it is, and speed costs money . . ." The SS454 that they tested had a sticker price of $4,852.30, which wasn't too far from the $5,192 base price of a 1970 Corvette.

Nineteen seventy was to the musclecar era what 1959 was to tail fins. After 1959, the fins shrunk; and after 1970, horsepower ratings declined. The change in 1959 occurred because the designers knew they had gone too far. The change in 1971 was due to pressure on the auto industry from the government agencies and the insurance companies. As a result of those forces, several modifications were made to the content of the 1971 Chevelle Super Sport. The brutal performance levels of the 1970 SS Chevelles were starting to wane. Chevrolet tried to stuff the genie back into the bottle by offering a selection of much smaller engines in the Super Sport.

Chevrolet dropped the 450-horsepower LS6 rating to 425 horsepower in 1971. Then in May 1971, the engine was dropped from Chevelle's option list. There is some speculation that none of the 425-

The 1970 Chevelle Super Sport was offered in two forms, the SS396 or the SS454. The only exterior difference was the addition of three little numbers under the SS on the fender. Under the hood, the lowest horsepower 396 (402 ci) was rated at 350 horsepower and the highest horsepower 454 was rated at 450. In 1970, when an SS454, like this one, pulled into the local drive-in restaurant, it drew a crowd like a fight in a schoolyard.

On the rear of the 1970 Super Sport, an SS emblem was added to the right-hand side of the black rubber bumper insert. Rectangular taillights, with integral back-up lights, were set into the ends of the bumper. All SS models had bright twin exhaust tips.

The instrument panel for the SS Chevelle was unique. It featured three large round dials that housed the tachometer, speedometer, and clock. Three smaller gauges monitored fuel, amps, and temperature. Set into the center of the steering wheel was a small SS emblem. Looking out through the windshield, the driver could see the cowl induction door open.

horsepower 454s actually made it into production in the 1971 model year. The LS5 454 was rated at 365 horsepower in 1971, a five-horsepower increase over the 1970 version of the engine. Also available in the 1971 Chevelle SS was one version of the 402-ci engine (the former 396), now named the Turbo Jet 400 and rated at 300 horsepower. Chevrolet also added two versions of the 350-ci small block to the option list for the Chevelle SS: a two-barrel equipped model, rated at 270 horsepower and a four-barrel version, rated at 300 horsepower. The compression ratios on all the 1971 engines were drastically dropped to meet the federal mandate to run on low lead fuel. Big blocks were reduced to 9.0:1 and small blocks to 8.5:1.

There were only two transmission selections for a 454-equipped 1971 SS Chevelle: an M-22 heavy-duty four-speed manual or the Turbo Hydra-Matic 400. The Turbo Jet 400 and 350 engines were standard with a three-speed manual transmission. Optional were an M-20 wide-ratio four-speed and either a Turbo Hydra-Matic 350 or 400. All three-speed manual transmissions were floor-shifted, except the one that backed the two-barrel equipped 350, which was column-shifted.

The exterior appearance of the 1971 Chevelle Super Sport changed very little from the 1970

Two different engines could be found under the hood of an SS454: the base 360-horsepower LS5 or the 450-horsepower LS6—the ultimate muscle-car engine. All 1970 Super Sport Chevelles had chrome-accented engines. This LS5 version has the special air cleaner, with a black-painted lid, that mates to the cowl induction hood.

LS6 Turbo Jet 454 - 450

The greatest of all time. In hockey, it was the 1980 U.S. Olympic ice hockey team's win over the USSR. In baseball, it's any New York Yankee team from the 1950s. And in boxing, it's Mohammed "I am the greatest" Ali. When it comes to Chevy Super Sport engines, the greatest has to be the 1970 454-ci LS6. Although there were other monster Chevy engines available through the COPO back door, none of them were listed in a sales brochure. In 1970, any Joe could walk into a local Chevy dealer and order an SS Chevelle with the full-on, ground-pounding kick-anybody's-ass-on-the-street 450-horsepower LS6. Records show that 4,475 customers plunked down the extra $263.30 to own a bona fide piece of history. Those who ordered the LS6 had only two transmission options—an M22 close-ratio four-speed or a heavy-duty Turbo Hydra-Matic 400. Hats off to those brave souls who endured astronomical insurance rates and 10 miles per gallon. For those interested in numbers, here are the specs.

Rated Horsepower	450 @ 5,600 rpm
Rated Torque	500 lb-ft @ 3,600 rpm

Engine Suffix Code	CRV: Four-speed CRR: Turbo Hydra-Matic 400
Bore x Stroke	4.25 x 4.00 inches
Compression ratio	11.25:1
Carburetor	Single Holley 800-cfm 4150 series, part number 3767477
Intake Manifold	Aluminum dual plane
Camshaft duration	Intake: 316 degrees Exhaust: 302 degrees
Camshaft lift	.52-inch Intake & Exhaust
Lifters	Mechanical
Valve lash	Intake: 0.024 inch Exhaust: 0.028 inch
Valve diameter	Intake: 2.19 inch Exhaust: 1.88 inch
Pushrods	3/8-inch diameter
Crankshaft	Forged steel
Pistons	Forged aluminum
Engine Block	Cast iron, four-bolt mains

model. Up front, the quad headlights were replaced with a pair of larger 7-inch-diameter headlights. In the rear, four circular taillights were inset into the bumper, replacing the rectangular taillights. The sides of the front fenders, along with the center of the grille and rear bumper, all featured SS emblems. The domed hood was standard with the SS option. Stripes and cowl induction were optional. One addition to the 1971 SS was a new set of 15x7-inch, argent gray five-spoke, stamped-steel wheels that came as standard equipment with either Goodyear or Firestone F70-15 tires plus bright outer trim rings.

Mid-1971, a new Chevelle option was released-the Heavy Chevy. It was Chevrolet's response to Plymouth's bare bones Road Runner. The Heavy Chevy had the same domed hood and blacked-out grille as the SS. Added were side stripes and Heavy Chevy decals and Rally Wheels. Any V-8 was available except for the 454. The stripped-down

SS was continued into the 1972 model year, but it never reached the soul of Chevy lovers the way the SS models did.

The 1972 Chevelle SS was identical to the 1971 model, with a few minor mechanical changes. The engine compartment took the biggest hit as the 454's horsepower rating dropped to 270 horsepower, the 400's rating to 240 horsepower, and the two 350s to 175 and 165 horsepower. A 307-ci small block was now the standard engine with its 130 horsepower. It should be noted that all of the 1972 ratings were net horsepower ratings. This system of rating was adopted industrywide and gave more consistent and realistic horsepower numbers for all cars.

Also on the government's hit list of fun items was the convertible. Convertibles were seen as unsafe and were targeted for the possible inclusion of roll bars. Consumers also shied away from them because they were prone to vandalism and theft. Air conditioning and sun roofs quickly became the re-

In 1971, Chevrolet released the Heavy Chevy option, which was a stripped-down version of the Chevelle SS. The Heavy Chevy had its own unique stripes and Rally Wheels, but used the same domed hood and blacked-out grille as the Super Sport Chevelle. Like the SS Chevelle, it was offered with a wide selection of V-8s, except the 454, which remained exclusive for the Super Sport. Pictured here are the 1972 versions of the Heavy Chevy (left) and the Super Sport Chevelle. *Copyright 1978–1999 GM Corp. Used with permission of GM Media Archives*

In 1971, the only external changes on the SS Chevelle, other than the headlights and taillights, were the new 15-inch stamped-steel wheels that resembled five-spoke mags. Under the hood, Chevy cut the LS6, leaving only one 454, rated at 365 horsepower, and one 396 rated at 300. This reduction in horsepower was due to the requirement for low-lead fuel. *Copyright 1978–1999 GM Corp. Used with permission of GM Media Archives*

The 1973 Chevelle was originally scheduled for the 1972 model year, but the crippling 1970 UAW strike against General Motors pushed its release back by one year. The new Chevelle featured a wheelbase of 113 inches, 1 inch longer than the 1972 model. The suspension was refined and front disc brakes were standard on all models.

placement for the folding top. The last Chevelle Super Sport convertible was a 1972 model.

In 1973, the Chevelle was completely restyled. This car was originally scheduled for the 1972 model year, but the crippling 1970 United Automobile Workers (UAW) strike against General Motors pushed design and engineering schedules back by one year. The new Chevelle shared its basic body with the other General Motors A-body intermediates, as well as the redesigned Monte Carlo. It featured a wheelbase of 113 inches, 1 inch longer than the 1972 model. The suspension was refined and front disc brakes were standard. The new Chevelle was 5.4 inches longer and 1 inch wider than the 1972 models, with most of the added length coming from the jutting 5-mile-per-hour front bumper, which along with its massive structure and the shock absorbers behind it, added considerable weight to the front of the car.

The 1973 Chevelle body was a clean design with an attractive fastback roof on the two-door models. This roof included a thick B-pillar and fixed quarter windows. These concessions were made for the rollover standards. Both the front and rear wheel openings were full and had a large, flared lip. The sides of the body had lots of what designers call "tumble home," which is where the sides of the body tuck under at the lower edges. Keeping with the clean design were flush, new, exterior door handles. Between the two large headlights was a grille consisting of a series of thin horizontal bars. The quad taillights resembled those of the 1972 model, except they were moved up, off of the bumper, onto a rear panel. In 1973, the rear bumper also came under the scrutiny of the federal government and was designed to take a 2-1/2-mile-per-hour hit.

The Super Sport option (Z15 for $242.50) was available on the two-door coupe and two station

Chevy Smog Hardware

One of the environmental consequences of the industrial revolution has been the weakening of the gaseous envelope around our planet. Beginning in the late 1950s, the problem was worsening and those concerned with the long-term health of our atmosphere started to pinpoint areas where improvement could be made. In addition to what rose from the smokestacks in large industrial complexes, the noxious gasses emitted from automobile tailpipes were carefully scrutinized.

The problem of auto exhaust emissions was one of the areas targeted by the State of California, where air quality in the Los Angeles basin was especially toxic. The first emission device approved by the California State Motor Vehicle Pollution Control Board was GM's PCV (positive crankcase ventilator) valve. The PCV was developed by the AC Spark Plug Division to reduce hydrocarbons (HC), one of the major components of auto exhaust emissions. It was a simple valve that recycled crankcase gasses into the intake manifold. Even though the PCV was virtually foolproof and extremely effective, it was derided by auto enthusiasts. The PCV was a required option on all 1962 Chevys sold in California and soon after became standard on all GM cars.

California's stiffer emission requirements once again led the way when, in 1966, all cars sold in that state were required to be fitted with an AIR (air injection reactor) pump. The AIR pump was about the size of an alternator and, like the alternator, was a belt-driven accessory. It functioned as a small air compressor, pumping fresh air through a series of tubes into the exhaust manifolds. The increase of oxygen in the manifold helped to burn off additional amounts of hydrocarbon. Even though the AIR pump drew a maximum of 10 horsepower, it was seen as the Antichrist by performance enthusiasts, and many of the original pumps were quickly exorcised from the engine compartment.

In 1970, Chevrolet added TCS (Transmission Controlled Spark) to help control HC emissions. TCS was activated only when the transmission, manual or automatic, was in any gear other than high. In all the other forward gears, vacuum to the distributor's vacuum advance unit was interrupted. An electric cut-off valve, signaled from a switch on and controlled by the transmission, retarded the spark by eliminating the vacuum advance. Also in 1970, California required an evaporative emission system that trapped fuel vapors that would have normally been dispersed into the atmosphere.

Along with the above mentioned hardware, the 1970s saw a reduction in compression ratios, revised ignition timing advance, the addition of the EGR (exhaust gas recirculator), an increase in thermostat temperatures, recalibrated carburetors with limited adjustment capabilities, catalytic converters, and the resultant requirement of unleaded gasoline. It wasn't until the 1980s that fuel injection was added to accurately control the air/fuel mixture. New engines were developed for the Super Sport Chevys of the 1990s that offered performance levels of the 1960s, the driveability of a luxury sedan, the fuel economy of an import, and exhaust emission levels believed unattainable 30 years earlier.

This 1967 Chevelle SS396 has the optional 375-horsepower engine. On the top of the engine is an AIR (air injection reactor) pump. The AIR pump was a belt-driven accessory that pumped fresh air through a series of hoses and tubes directly into the exhaust manifolds. The increased oxygen in the manifold helped to burn off excess hydrocarbons. First installed on California cars in 1966, the AIR pump was soon seen on cars delivered in all states.

In 1973, the Chevelle two-door had an attractive fastback roof. Federal rollover standards dictated the thick B-pillars and fixed quarter windows. Super Sport models had lower body side and wheel opening stripes. G70-14 white letter tires on 14x7-inch wide Rally Wheels were standard on the SS. The large rear bumper was required to meet federal 2 1/2-mile-per-hour standards.

wagon models (a one-year only option, thank goodness). The SS option consisted of a blacked-out grille with an SS emblem in the center, dual sport mirrors, lower body side and wheel opening stripes, black accented taillight bezels, front fender and rear panel SS emblems, and bright quarter window moldings. Super Sports rolled on 14x7-inch wide Rally Wheels fitted with G70-14 white letter tires. On the interior there was a special instrument cluster with SS badges in the center of the steering wheel and on the door panels. A bench seat was standard, but sexy swiveling bucket seats were optional.

Three engines were available in the 1973 Super Sport Chevelle: two 350s rated at 145 or 175 horsepower, and a single 454 rated at 245 horsepower. The vehicle's engine displacement was designated by a small emblem above the front fender's side marker light. A three-speed manual was standard on the 350s with optional four-speed manual or Turbo Hydra-Matic. The 454 came with either a four-speed or Turbo Hydra-Matic.

Nineteen seventy-three was the year of the first OPEC oil shortage and, coincidentally, the last year for the SS Chevelle. The Laguna S3 would soldier on, trying to fly the performance flag for the Chevelle, but it didn't have the undeniable style of the Super Sport models and it certainly didn't have the all-out performance of those mighty big blocks of 1969 and 1970. The Chevelle Super Sport models have gone down in history as one of the best automotive combinations of style, size, and performance ever built. They will forever be an icon of the musclecar era.

The 1967 Camaro was Chevrolet's delayed response to the Ford Mustang. It offered the same long-hood, short-deck design as the Mustang and matched it option for option. The 1967 Camaro was built in two body styles, a coupe and a convertible. Chevy also had the foresight to include an SS option for the new Camaro. Transverse stripes on the nose and twin hood vents were part of the Super Sport package.

Chapter 5

Camaro SS
Chevy's Amazing Pony Car

When Ford introduced the new Mustang in April 1964, Chevrolet's management team stood back to watch and wait. They were anxious to see the public's response to Ford's new pony car. They were also confident that the completely restyled 1965 Corvair, scheduled to be released in the fall of 1964, would fill any vacuum created by the Mustang. Everyone—even Ford executives—underestimated the instant and immense response to the Mustang. It was a reasonably priced sporty car with a conventional driveline and chassis. Even though it was based on the Falcon platform, it didn't have the Falcon's stodgy look. The Mustang's long list of options gave the customer the opportunity to order an affordable car of his or her dreams. Nineteen sixty-four also saw the release of Ralph Nader's book, *Unsafe at Any Speed*. New Corvairs—now seen as a pariah—sat unsold on the showroom floors. The combination of the hot selling Mustang and the Corvair's death spiral produced a cold chill within Chevrolet's executive offices. There was only one solution: build a simple sporty car—the Camaro.

During a press luncheon at the New York International Auto Show in May 1966, Chevrolet General Manager Pete Estes was asked if Chevrolet would have a Mustang-type car in 1967, and, if so, what would it be called? Estes let the proverbial cat out of the bag with one word, "Panther." Panther was the code name for the new car Chevrolet was developing for the sporty car market. Estes wouldn't make any predictions on first year sales, but he guaranteed the new car would be competitive. The Panther was renamed and released in 1967 as the Camaro.

Bill Mitchell loved sporty cars, which to him meant sexy, curvy lines; bucket seats; a performance engine; a floor shift; and a maximum seating capacity of four. It had always been his desire to build a four-place sporty car, but the time had never been right. Still, he had had at least one designer working on such a car since 1962, which was how the Corvair Monza was conceived. The Corvair's demise and the success of the Mustang gave Mitchell his chance to design a breed of car he favored.

Mitchell envisioned the new Camaro as a four-passenger Corvette. It would deviate from the Mustang's angular proportions—squared off top, short rear deck, and long front end. Instead, the Camaro would have a more rounded look with voluptuous curves. Mitchell's enthusiasm for cars was reflected by the staff he selected. Designing cars was more than a job—it was a passion. Coming in, they knew not every project they worked on would be a Corvette, after all, the majority of Chevrolet's line was bread-and-butter cars. So when the opportunity came along to do a car like the Camaro, they were excited. "The guys in the studio were fired up with the opportunity to do the Camaro—it was a whole new animal," former General Motors Design Vice President Chuck Jordan recalls with a smile. "People imagine these ideas and if you're revved up and excited about a project, these things start to come out. You wake up at night with ideas; you don't wake up and think about Chevy IIs."

The shape of the new Camaro was created in Henry Haga's Chevrolet Studio No. 2. The inspiration came from a show car called the Super Nova, which was displayed at the 1964 New York Auto

Slender bumpers in the rear of the 1967 Camaro added to the illusion of width. Simple rectangular taillights were placed on a flat rear panel with the gas filler cap in between. When the Super Sport option was selected, an SS-emblazoned cap was used.

Show. The Super Nova emphasized roundness and fluidity, a trademark of mid-1960s Chevrolet design.

Henry Haga, in the book *Camaro Style, Speed, and Spirit*, spoke about the design of the Camaro: "We felt very strongly about reducing design to its simplest form, using only one peak down each body side, interrupted by accented wheel arches. The profile of the car also was very simple, using the classic approach of crowned fender lines, with their high points directly above the accented wheel arches. We purposefully avoided any contrived design lines and superfluous detail. Even the execution of the wide, horizontal loop front end and grille, with its hidden headlamps in the Rally Sport variant, was as pure in concept as we could make it."

Slender bumpers fore and aft restated the theme of simplicity and gave the illusion of added width. The headlights were single units placed in the corners of the oval grille, and the taillight assemblies

were simple, two-segment horizontal units with a gas filler in between.

Chevrolet designers made the interior package dimensions for the Camaro similar to those of the Mustang. The Camaro was only 1.3 inches longer than the Mustang, as well as slightly lower and wider. The 1967 Camaro was to be built in only two body styles, a coupe and a convertible. A two-seat convertible and a fastback model similar to the Mustang 2+2 had each been proposed, but neither was approved.

The 1967 Camaro's instrument panel had two large circular instruments on a receding surface in front of the driver. This design would reappear in 1968 in the Corvette. Controls were placed high on the instrument panel and with all edges rounded off to protect the occupants in case of an accident. In the center were the heater and radio controls, both recessed for safety. The center of the instrument panel

Chevrolet's new 350-ci small block, rated at 295 horsepower, was available only on the Camaro in 1967. This was the only small block available in a 1967 SS Camaro. All SS Camaros in 1967 had chrome engine accents.

swept down into a console that divided the two front bucket seats. The Camaro's small rear seats were no larger than those on the Mustang. The Camaro's deluxe interior used foam-backed molded door panels, which was similar to the design introduced on the 1965 Corvette. Chevrolet engineers applied new technology to the low-production Corvette to prove out components and methods before installing them on a large production run.

To reduce engineering time and cost, many of the Camaro's basic components were off-the-shelf technology. The cowl, front subframe, and rear suspension were all borrowed from the 1968 Nova. The decision to use the Nova's cowl was controversial. Its height restricted the overall design by raising the center of the car more than Mitchell and his designers had wanted. Chevy's designers also wanted the front wheel stretched out farther forward like the Mustang, but they were restricted by the Nova's subframe and its relation to the cowl.

Above and right
On the 1967 Camaro, Chevrolet offered a Rally Sport (RS) option that featured hidden headlights. The blending of the RS and SS options created a stunning combination.

Chevrolet engineers gained a great deal of experience in unitized body design with the Corvair and Chevy II. The new Camaro's body was a unitized design with the addition of a front subframe (the same design would appear on the 1968 Nova). A subframe is a partial chassis frame used to hold suspension components, and, in the case of a front subframe like that of the Camaro, the engine. The subframe is mounted to the body with rubber biscuits to isolate engine and road noise and vibration. The 1967 Camaro was Chevrolet's first experience with a subframe design.

Chevrolet led the way in 1967 with a wide array of stylish performance cars. At the head of the pack was the new Camaro SS, followed closely by an SS427 Impala, an SS396 Chevelle, a Nova SS, and a 427 Corvette. With a young man behind the wheel of each of these cars, the target market was obvious. The photo could also be interpreted as "Drive one of these cars and you'll get the pretty girl." *Copyright 1978–1999 GM Corp. Used with permission of GM Media Archives*

In the early 1960s, Bill Jenkins made a name for himself tuning the Chevys that Dave Strickler drove. After a short stint racing Mopars, Jenkins returned to the Chevy camp as both driver and tuner of a 396-powered 1967 Camaro. While Jenkins' car is not marked as an SS, it was the only way a big block could be purchased in a Camaro. *1996, NHRA Photographic*

For auto shows, Chevrolet often built cut-away versions of its cars. This 1968 Camaro SS has been sliced and diced to show patrons a complete view of normally hidden body structure and mechanical components. Early production SS Camaros, like this one, featured transverse nose stripes similar to those on the 1967 models. *Copyright 1978–1999 GM Corp. Used with permission of GM Media Archives*

Budget and time constraints limited the design of a new rear suspension for the Camaro, so the Chevy II's axle and single-leaf springs were installed. This rear suspension system was borderline on the Nova, and when the Camaro's V-8 power was applied, it highlighted the marginal design. Traction bars were added in an attempt to lessen rear wheel hop.

The base price of a 1967 Camaro coupe stickered for just under $2,500. Like the Mustang, the Camaro buyer could choose from a long list of factory and dealer options. In the end, a new Mustang and a new Camaro, similarly equipped, were within a few dollars of each other.

Chevrolet borrowed the 140-horsepower six-cylinder engine from the Chevelle as the standard engine for the Camaro. The 250-ci 155-horsepower six-cylinder engine from the full-size Chevy was optional. Both of these engines were standard with a three-speed manual transmission and available with the Powerglide automatic.

Like the Mustang, the new Camaro had a broad selection of V-8 engine options. The smallest V-8 was a 210-horsepower two-barrel carbureted 327-ci engine. The horsepower of the 327 jumped to 275 with the addition of a four-barrel carburetor and an increase in the compression ratio to 10.0:1. Available only on the Camaro in 1967 was Chevrolet's new 350-ci small block, rated at 295 horsepower. This served as the base engine when the Super Sport option was ordered and was the only small block available in a 1967 SS Camaro.

In 1967, Ford added its 390-ci V-8 to the Mustang option list. Chevrolet countered that move on the Camaro with two versions of the 396-ci engine. The smaller of the two was the 325-horsepower hydraulic lifter version that was the standard engine in the SS396 Chevelle and optional in the full-size Chevrolet. Also available for the Camaro was the L78 375-horsepower version—the same engine that was optional in the SS396 Chevelle. All Camaro V-8 engines came standard with a three-speed manual transmission or were available with an optional four-speed manual. Two automatic transmissions were available, as well: a Powerglide for the six-cylinder engines and small block V-8s, and a Turbo Hydra-Matic for the 325-horsepower 396 only.

The long list of options available for the Camaro made for some interesting combinations and little likelihood of seeing two identical cars. There were two Super Sport options for the 1967 Camaro and they were both tied to performance engines. The SS350 was option code L48. For an additional $210.65, the customer received the new 295-horsepower, 350-ci V-8 engine; a unique hood with twin chrome simulated vents; a special transverse front paint stripe (in black or white only); redline tires on 14x6-inch wheels; SS emblems on the fenders; and SS350 emblems in the center of the grille, on the gas cap, and in the center of the steering wheel. The SS396 Camaro offered the same body and trim features as the SS350, except the SS emblems had no

reference to the engine size. On the front fenders of the SS396 Camaro was the same crossed-flag 396 emblem that was also used on big block-equipped Impalas and Chevelles. All 1967 Super Sport Camaros were equipped with dual exhaust, heavy-duty suspension, and chrome engine accents.

In 1967, Chevrolet introduced optional front disc brakes on all of its passenger cars except the Corvair. The calipers were a four-piston design and were similar to ones used on the Corvette. Power assist was not required with disc brakes in 1967, but those who opted for the nonpower discs found pedal pressures uncomfortably high. All Chevys equipped with disc brakes had the new Rally Wheel. It was also possible to order drum brakes with metallic linings.

One Camaro option that stirred up a lot of interest in 1967 was the Z28. Its heart was the high-performance 302-ci V-8, which was fitted with a solid lifter cam and large Holley carburetor. Chevrolet

In 1968, federal regulations required that side marker lights be added to all new vehicles. This 1968 Camaro SS also has the popular RS option that featured hidden headlights. The SS emblems in the grille and on the gas cap no longer displayed the engine size. Engine displacement for all engines was located on the front edge of the front fenders. The stripes shown on this SS model are the later versions that swept rearward, terminating at the rear edge of the door. *Copyright 1978–1999 GM Corp. Used with permission of GM Media Archives*

COPO (Central Office Production Order) cars were sneaking off the production lines in 1968. These cars were special combinations not listed in the sales literature. Entrepreneurs, like Don Yenko, used the COPO system to create a small fleet of specialty performance cars, like this 427-powered Camaro SS.

Chevrolet made no bones about the fact that the 1968 Camaro was the car for the man who wanted Corvette performance in a less expensive, but sporty package. The "Hugging Cousins" headline in the ad is derived from the "Hugger" nickname the Chevy marketing staff gave to the Camaro.

added a heavy-duty suspension and some racing stripes to the coupe body and the Z28 was born. Only 602 were built in 1967 and they had their teething problems against the Mustangs in Trans-Am competition, but the lessons learned on the track were fed back to Chevrolet's engineering staff, and the fixes for the race cars often resulted in improvements that benefited not only the Z28, but all future Camaros.

One of the many options that Chevrolet offered on the Camaro was the RS, or Rally Sport, option Z-22. The words "Rally Sport" led one to believe that this option would provide a ground-hugging suspension and fat tires, but, unfortunately, on the 1967 Camaro it was only a trim package. The RS option included parking lights mounted on the front valence

panel; a special grille; hidden headlights; lower body side moldings; wheel opening moldings; bright drip rail moldings; rear valence mounted back-up lights; and special RS emblems on the grille, fender, steering wheel, and gas filler cap. Chevrolet allowed the unique mix of RS and SS options on the same car. When so optioned, the Super Sport was the predominant of the two and all the exterior emblems would be SS. It was also possible to have a Z28 with the RS option and like the SS, the Z28 was the predominant of the two. Buyers, however, could not combine the Z28 and SS options.

Even though the Camaro came late to the pony car party, it was fully dressed and ready for fun. It fed the appetite of Chevy lovers who had been hungered by the forbidden fruit of the Mustang. At the dealership, it may have taken away a few sales from the floundering Chevy II. The 1967 Camaro sold 220,917 units in its first year, about half of what Ford's Mustang sold.

Only minor trim changes differentiated the 1968 Camaro from the 1967 model. The most noticeable

change was the addition of side marker lights that were simply small rectangular add-ons to the front fender and quarter panel. Vent windows were removed from all 1968 Camaros in a move that Chevrolet touted as a new design feature that improved sealing, reduced wind noise, increased visibility, and reduced theft. The lack of vent windows pleased the stylists who preferred the cleaner look, while the bean counters looked at the new side glass as a big cost savings per car. Unfortunately, many customers missed the simple convenience of the vent windows.

With the exception of the rear suspension, the Camaro chassis was carried over from 1967. Traction bars, which had been added to the V-8 models in 1967 as a quick fix for wheel hop, were removed and the single-leaf spring was replaced with a multi-leaf heavy-duty unit. To further shore up the rear axle, the rear shocks were staggered. Feedback from teams racing the Z28s in 1967 were responsible for chassis improvements on the 1968 models. The disc brake option now included a power boost and the

In 1969, Chevrolet revised the Camaro's sheet metal below the belt line. A slight flare was added to the reshaped wheel openings. These new wheel openings looked especially good with the brawny F70-14 white letter tires that were standard with the SS option. The SS stripe was now a hockey stick design that tapered back across the top of the front fender.

The 1969 Camaro Super Sport's base engine was the 350-ci small block rated at 300 horsepower, up 5 horsepower from 1968. Three optional 396-ci engines were available, rated at 325, 350, and 375 horsepower. This 350-horsepower version is heavily optioned with air conditioning, power steering, and power brakes. The small unit below the master cylinder is for the cruise control.

In 1969, Chevy added a new pair of chrome hood vents to the Super Sport Camaro, each having four simulated stacks. The combination of RS and SS options proved successful and was again available on the 1969 models. The revised front end required new headlight doors for the hidden headlights with the RS option. Three attractive horizontal windows were added to each door. All SS model Camaros had blacked-out grilles, except for the cars that were painted black.

metallic drum brakes were no longer available. Rear disc brakes were also added as an option to the 1968 Camaro, a first for Chevrolet in a passenger car.

Three distinct upgrade options to the base Camaro were available again in 1968: Z28, RS, and SS. Chevrolet also continued the combination of RS (with its distinctive hidden headlights) with either Z28 or SS options. Similar to the 1967 SS option, the 1968 SS package was based around a selection of performance V-8 engines, but in 1968 this selection expanded. The base engine was the 295-horsepower 350-ci small block. Backing it was a three-speed manual transmission. Optional were either a four-speed manual or Powerglide. The 325-horsepower 396 was also available. It came with a three-speed manual as the standard transmission. A four-speed manual was available, along with a Turbo Hydra-Matic. The Powerglide was not available with this engine. Added to the SS engine option list in 1968 was the L34, 350-horsepower 396. This was the same 350-horsepower engine that was used in the 1968 SS Chevelle and Nova. The 350-horsepower engine was available only with a four-speed manual or Turbo Hydra-Matic transmission. The L78,

375-horsepower 396 also returned for 1968. It was only available with a four-speed manual transmission. New for the 1968 Camaro SS was the L89 375-horsepower engine that was equipped with aluminum heads. The only transmission available for L78 and L89 engines was the close-ratio four-speed.

Along with one of Chevy's powerful engines, the SS option offered a special package of exterior trim. SS badges were placed in the grille, on the fender sides, and on the gas cap. None of these SS badges displayed a designation of engine size, however. All SS models had transverse front stripes that tapered back to a point at the rear edge of the door. Some of the early production 1968 Camaro SS models had the same front stripes as the 1967 SS models. Depending on the body color, these stripes were either black or white. The 1968 SS Camaros with a 350 engine featured the same chrome hood vents as the

1967 model, however, if a 396 was specified, the hood vents resembled eight small chrome vertical stacks. Exterior engine designations on the Super Sport were either a small chrome 350 or 396 (depending on engine) on the forward edge of the front fender. The SS models had upgraded front and rear springs, finned brake drums, red stripe F70-14 tires, and dual exhaust. When one of the big blocks was ordered, a set of heavy-duty shocks was added.

In 1968, new emphasis was given to the popular Z28 option. The Z28 proved to be an excellent car and Chevy's promotion of it had sales skyrocketing. This increase in Z28 sales did have a minor impact on the sales of the SS models. Overall sales for the Camaro's sophomore year were outstanding, with 235,151 units, with 30,695 of those optioned with one of the SS packages. Even though Chevy refined the Camaro, Ford's Mustang still outsold it, but by a much slimmer margin than in 1967.

Significant styling changes were introduced on the 1969 Camaro. While the previous models had been cleaner and smaller looking, the 1969 Camaro grew in bulk. Most noticeably was its larger grille opening and attractively flared fenders. The slender horizontal front bumper design now curled up on the ends, wrapping into the fender cap. Within the cavernous grille opening was the large grid egg-crate grille, joining at the center in a V shape. The Rally Sport option again offered hidden headlights, but now there were three horizontal windows in each headlight door. The taillights were similar to the 1967 and 1968 models, but were longer and thinner. In 1969, the Camaro and Nova shared the same instrument panel, but the Camaro's unique instrument cluster distinguished it from the Nova.

The revised sheet metal below the belt line on the 1969 Camaro was exceptionally well done. The front and rear wheel openings were flattened on the top, which changed their shape from round to rectangular. A slight flare was added that began at the front wheel opening's leading edge and swept back across the wheel opening, along the door, and onto

When a big block engine was ordered with a 1969 Camaro Super Sport, the rear taillight panel was painted black. The rear spoiler on this 1969 Super Sport Camaro was not a standard part of the SS option. It, along with a front spoiler, were an extra cost option that added $31 to the window sticker. Convertible tops were available in either black or white.

When a customer ordered a Super Sport Camaro in 1969 with the custom interior group (RPO Z87), it included molded vinyl door panels with built-in arm rests and carpeting on the lower edge, an assist grip on the doors, woodgrain accents on the instrument panel and steering wheel, bright pedal trim, and extra insulation. This SS is also equipped with a tilt wheel, stereo radio, and power windows.

the quarter panel. These new wheel openings looked especially good with the brawny F70-14 tires that were standard with the SS option.

Exterior identification for the 1969 Camaro Super Sport models included an SS emblem in the center of the grille, on the sides of the front fenders, and on the rear taillight panel. All 1969 SS Camaros, regardless of engine size, had twin chrome hood ornaments, each of which had four simulated carburetor stacks. The Super Sport stripes changed slightly for 1969. Instead of a band that wrapped over the nose and swept rearward, the new SS stripes were shaped like a hockey stick. From a wide vertical band on the forward edge of the front fender, a tapering stripe followed the top of the fender across the door where it ended at the door handle. These stripes were available in white, black, and red. There was also an optional set of SS stripes featuring a set of banded nose stripes that split at the center of the hood and tapered back to the hood's rear edge. The only interior SS identification was on the center of the steering wheel.

Chevrolet continued the performance engine-based musclecar theme in the 1969 SS Camaro. The base Super Sport 350-ci engine was bumped up to 300 horsepower and had four-bolt mains. The 396-ci engines, which were now increased to 402 cubic inches, were again rated at 325, 350, and 375 horsepower. As in 1968, there were two 375-horsepower versions with the difference being the cylinder head material, cast iron or aluminum.

A cowl induction hood was a new option on the 1969 Camaro. It was initially designed for race cars competing in the Trans-Am series. GM stylist Larry Shinoda penned the lines of the simple, raised rectangular area that swept back to the cowl where an electric solenoid opened a door allowing cool air to the carburetor. The hood's option number was ZL-2 and it was available for an additional $79 on the Super Sport or Z28 optioned models. Along with being functional, the new hood gave the Camaro an aggressive look and proved to be a popular option, with over 10,000 Camaros so optioned in 1969. Also new for the Camaro in 1969 was the body-color Endura front bumper.

For the second time in three years, the Chevrolet Camaro was selected to pace the Indianapolis 500. To commemorate the occasion, Chevrolet built 3,675 Pace Car replicas. The Pace Car was designed to be a

The 1969 Camaro instrument panel was the same as the Nova, except for a unique instrument cluster. This SS model is fitted with the optional woodgrain steering wheel and special instrumentation option U17. This package includes ammeter, temperature gauge, oil pressure, and fuel gauges mounted on the console. In the instrument cluster, a tach and clock are added.

convertible, but a few coupes were built. All Pace Cars were Super Sport models combined with the RS option, and all were painted Dover White with Hugger Orange stripes and orange houndstooth interiors. All Pace Cars were equipped with the new cowl induction hood and Rally Wheels.

Sales were good for the Camaro in 1969 with a total of 243,095 units sold. This included over 35,000 Super Sports and over 20,000 Z28s. It must be noted that due to labor strikes, the sales of the 1969 Camaro were extended into the 1970 model year.

When the new Camaros (destined to be known also as 1970-1/2 models) were finally released in the spring of 1970, the Camaro fans were presented with a car that had been dramatically restyled. Bill Mitchell had to live with many compromises that affected the look of the first generation Camaro. Now that there wasn't the pressure to get a car (to compete with the Mustang) to market, Mitchell had the time to finesse the exact look he wanted. The Camaro's sales numbers also justified a unique platform (F-body) for the 1970 Camaro and its clone, the

Firebird. No longer restricted to share body components, Mitchell's designers were given the freedom to explore some radical alternatives.

The second-generation Camaro was designed as a coupe. At that time, very little consideration was given to building a convertible, since sales of convertibles were trailing off and the government was threatening new rollover standards that would be difficult to meet. In addition, more people were ordering air conditioning as an option. The new Camaro's roofline was a fastback design that gracefully tapered into the short rear deck. Up front, there were two large high-set headlights. The grille was rectangular in shape with an egg-crate mesh. A thin blade bumper bisected the grille and gently wrapped around onto the fender edges. On the valence panel below the bumper, two large rectangular parking lights were positioned below the headlights. From the top of the grille, a raised section swept back across the hood, washing out at the rear edge. Under the rear edge of the long hood were the hidden wipers. Down the middle of each side was a

When the SS option was ordered in 1969, the simulated louvers in front of the rear wheel were trimmed in chrome and the rocker panels were painted black. The luggage rack on the deck lid was a dealer option.

In 1969, a Chevy Camaro was selected to pace the Indianapolis 500 race. Chevrolet produced a special model based on a Super Sport and RS combination. The Pace Car accents were added with option Z-11. All 1969 Camaro Pace Cars were Dover White with Hugger Orange stripes. They were all fitted with the cowl induction hood and orange houndstooth interiors. The Indy Pace Car in this particular photo is missing the front fender engine designation. *Copyright 1978–1999 GM Corp. Used with permission of GM Media Archives*

pronounced character line that defined the crown in the Camaro's side. This line was interrupted only by the slightly flared lip on the top of each wheel opening. The passenger doors were long and featured frameless side glass and flush exterior handles. The rear of the new Camaro was a simple flat panel with two pairs of large circular lights at each end. In the center of the panel was a depression for the license plate. The rear bumper was as thin as the one on the front. It had a dip in the center for the license plate and, at each end, it curved up to meet and blend into the rear edge of the quarter panel. On a scale of 1 to 10, the new Camaro was a 10-plus—Bill Mitchell had done it again.

While the entire body was changed, Chevrolet didn't dare change the content of its most popular performance options. The Z28, Super Sport, and RS packages were each still available. The Super Sport option consisted of a blacked-out grille, dual sport mirrors, SS emblems in the center of the grille and rear panel. Super Sport emblems were also located on

the sides of the front fenders. Below these SS emblems were small engine designation emblems, either 350 or 396, depending on the engine option selected. When a 396 engine was selected, the rear taillight panel was painted black. All 1970 SS Camaros were equipped with 14x7-inch wheels and F70-14 white letter tires. Included with the SS option were power front disc brakes, F41 heavy-duty suspension option, and chrome exhaust tips. In 1970, there were no stripes available as part of the SS option.

As in previous years, the SS option could be combined with the RS option. In 1970, the RS option included a split front bumper, which fully exposed the grille, and a body-colored urethane grille surround. Dave Holls was the chief designer in the Chevrolet studio when the 1970 Camaro was designed. "The greatest thing in the world was when we had the guts to move up to the GTO-type bumpers," exclaims Holls. "I never thought we'd ever get that into production. We couldn't afford a full Endura front like Pontiac. That was like an $85

In 1970, Chevrolet introduced an entirely new Camaro. Because it was no longer required to share its platform with the Nova, Chevy's designers were free to develop an exciting design without making compromises for another vehicle. Chevrolet continued the RS/SS combination on the Camaro. In 1970, the RS option created an exotic look with the split front bumpers and special Endura nose piece. The Z28 style stripes on this 1970 Super Sport Camaro were not part of the SS option.

deal and that would have put us out of our price class with Mustang. So we had one luxury model where we tried to get away with it—and it went! That one model was my absolute favorite Camaro. We were proud of that car! That was a beautiful body and what a roaring success that F-body was."

When the Super Sport option was selected in 1970, the standard engine was the 300-horsepower 350. Two 396 engines were optional, rated at 350 and 375 horsepower. Camaro, like all the other Chevy lines using the 396 engine, continued to refer to it as a 396 even though it had grown to 402

cubic inches. Super Sport customers had the choice of either a four-speed manual or a Turbo Hydra-Matic transmission.

In 1970, the pony car reached full maturity. Every manufacturer, including American Motors, had one, but Chevy's Camaro led the pack with affordable performance and advanced styling. But, the musclecar era was about to flatline and no one in the industry was reaching for the paddles to revive it. Federal requirements for lower exhaust emissions and safer body and interior design filled the engineers' plates, leaving them no choice when it came to the question of whether to keep horsepower high or reduce exhaust emissions.

The first casualties of the emission and insurance onslaught appeared in 1971 when Chevrolet offered only two engines for the Camaro Super Sport models: the base 350-ci engine rated at 270 horsepower and the only optional big block, rated at 300 horsepower. Lower compression ratios were responsible for the reduction in horsepower.

The exterior of the 1971 Super Sport Camaro was almost identical to that of the 1970 models. Only minor changes in emblem design and paint

Displaying cut-away models was the fashionable thing to do at auto shows in 1970. This 1970 Camaro SS was dissected for this display. It gave auto show patrons a good look at the mechanical workings of the car, but unfortunately destroyed the overall look of a beautifully styled car. *Copyright 1978–1999 GM Corp. Used with permission of GM Media Archives*

In 1971, the Camaro Super Sport 396 big block engine (actual cubic-inch displacement was 402) was rated at 300 horsepower. In 1972 that rating was dropped to 240 horsepower. In 1973, both the Super Sport option and big block engine were dropped from the Camaro. *Chris Richardson*

colors differentiated the new models from the 1970 versions. The same was true for the interior, except for new high-back bucket seats.

In 1972, General Motors and the rest of the auto industry revised the way engine power output was rated, by adopting the SAE net horsepower system. With this new system, the 1972 Camaro Super Sport base 350-ci engine was now rated at 200 horsepower, and the optional 402 (still marketed as a 396) was rated at 240 horsepower. The exterior of the 1972 SS-optioned Camaro was the same as in 1971. It was obvious that little effort was being put into increasing the performance level of the Camaro.

Nineteen seventy-two would be the last year for the Super Sport Camaro. It, along with all the other performance cars, died a slow death and no one seemed to care. In 1972, sales of the SS Camaros fell to 6,562 and only 2,757 Z28 optioned Camaros were sold. At that time, it was hard to imagine that anyone would ever want a high-performance car again.

An entire generation of Americans would be born, raised, and well into their careers before another Camaro Super Sport would be available at a Chevy dealer. In 1996, Chevrolet released a contemporary version of Camaro SS. This new Super Sport was an option on the fourth-generation Camaro,

which had been introduced in 1993. The new 1993 Camaro was as stunning to the public as the 1970 Camaro had been. Once again, General Motors' designers produced a car with distinctive styling.

In a world awash with front-wheel-drive cars, Chevrolet product planners had the unusual foresight and courage to continue the rear-wheel-drive configuration for the new Camaro. It was also kept in a four-seat configuration.

The styling of the new Camaro was based on a concept car that was built at General Motors' West Coast Advanced Concept center in Newbury Park, California. The "California Camaro" was a sleek design that resembled a watermelon seed with a bump on top. The long hood swept down to a pointed nose that had a large grille opening underneath. "Cat's eye" headlights were silhouetted into the leading edge of the hood and front fender. Sweeping up from the top of the front fender was a fairing that blended into the rearview mirror's housing on the door. The roof was a smallish bubble added to the body. It was distinguished by a severely raked windshield and wide C-pillar. The rear deck was short and well rounded, and a full-width spoiler and cat's eye-shaped taillights completed the rear end treatment. Looking back, it's undeniable that this was the new Camaro.

The 1993 Camaro retained the 101-inch wheelbase. The exterior dimensions grew slightly, but this expansion was unapparent because of no hard defining lines in the body. From a distance the new Camaro looked smaller than its predecessor. But, parked next to another car, its overall size was obvious.

When designing a new car, it's much easier to package required components than trying to retrofit an older design. Chevrolet took the opportunity with the 1993 Camaro to add dual air bags and CFC-free refrigerant to the air conditioner—both of these would soon be a federal requirement. Chevrolet was able to tout these additions as features of the new models to an environmentally and safety conscious consumer base. ABS was another standard feature added to the new Camaro.

Since the mid-1980s, Ford's 302-powered Mustang has held court as the modern day musclecar. It was inexpensive and had outstanding acceleration. Ford also relished the attention the Mustang received in its role as a police pursuit vehicle. Police vehicle requirements extended beyond acceleration into areas of engine cooling, handling, and braking. The Mustang continually improved and was the vehicle of choice for many departments, including the California Highway Patrol. Chevrolet had a police package for the Camaro, but it wasn't until 1993 that it was refined enough to compete head-to-head with the Mustang. Many of the components that Chevrolet developed for police package Camaros were placed into production for the 1993 Z28.

With the exception of 1975 and 1976, Chevrolet had continued to offer the Z28 option on the Camaro (in 1988 and 1989, the Z28 came in the form of the IROC-Z). The Z28 continued to carry the Camaro's high-performance banner all those years. When the 1993 model was introduced, the Z28 once again looked and performed like a musclecar. Under the hood was the Camaro version of the Corvette LT1 rated at 275 horsepower. Cost constraints dictated two bolt mains, a single catalytic converter, and the lack of other underhood cosmetics. This engine was stout enough to push the new Camaro through the quarter mile in 14 seconds flat at 100 miles per hour—an elapsed time and speed that would warm the heart of a 1960s-era musclecar lover. This level of performance was a notch higher than the Mustang, a point Chevy lovers never failed to mention.

In 1994, after a 24-year absence, a convertible was added to the Camaro. Times and tastes change, and members of the auto-buying public again wanted to feel the wind in their hair. The convertible option in 1994 was expensive. It added an additional $5,000 to the cost of the car.

In 1996 Chevrolet added an SS model. This latest version offered more than a trim package. In fact, it produced performance levels equal to or better than 1960s-era big block Camaros. It was designed for a 1990's market to attract buyers who might be looking at a Mustang Cobra or GT. The new SS, which, by the way, was not designated as a Super Sport, but only as an SS, was an option to the Z28 performance package. At $3,999, the SS option wasn't inexpensive. For the extra money the customer received the 305-horsepower 5.7-liter engine, a composite hood with a

continued on page 111

NEXT PAGE
When Chevrolet redesigned the Camaro in 1993, the only performance package offered was the Z28. Its performance level was still high enough to beat its perennial competition—the Ford Mustang. In 1996, Chevy upped the performance of the Z28 with the addition of the SS package. Designed and installed by SLP (Street Legal Performance), it considerably increased the performance levels of the already quick Camaro Z28.

The 1972 Camaro was the last of the second-generation models to have a Super Sport option available. The exterior markings were minimal, especially when combined with the RS option. *Chris Richardson*

SLP's modifications to the exterior of the 1996 Z28 were simple, but effective. The ZR-1 style 17x9-inch alloy wheels, fitted with 275/40 ZR17 BFGoodrich Comp TA tires, nestled perfectly in the sleek Camaro's wheel openings. On the side of each front fender, right where they were located decades ago, SLP placed a small SS emblem.

functional hood scoop that provided forced air induction to the engine, a revised rear deck spoiler, BFGoodrich Comp TA 275/40ZR17 tires on special 9-inch wide wheels (convertibles were fitted with 245/50ZR16 tires on 8-inch wheels), the coupes received a Level I suspension upgrade that included a larger front antisway bar and a rear track bar (convertibles retained the standard Z28 suspension), Quaker State SynQuest synthetic engine oil, a numbered console plaque, and three-dimensional SS badges that replaced the Z28 badges on the front fenders and rear taillight panel.

The 1996 SS Camaro also offered additional performance upgrades only available on the SS. For $349, a Hurst shifter was available for the six-speed manual transmission. A low-restriction exhaust system was available for an additional $499. It was an all stainless-steel system that used larger-diameter pipes. This exhaust system increased the engine's horsepower to 310. For $999, a Level II suspension could be specified. It offered specially valved front and rear Bilstein shocks and progressive rate springs. With this option, the rear lower control

The rectangular unit in the rear of the engine compartment is where the Camaro SS's hood scoop mated to the induction system. This 1996 Camaro SS's 5.7-liter engine thumped out a solid 305 horsepower. With the optional low-restriction exhaust system, that amount was increased to 310. Car and Driver ran a new 1996 SS down the quarter and stopped the clocks at 13.6 seconds, while running a speed of 106 miles per hour—times that were better than a 1960s-era big block Camaro.

For 1998, Chevy redesigned the headlights and front fascia of the Camaro. This new front end was carried into the 1999 model. The 320-horsepower LS1 engine that powered 1999 SS Camaros was also stingy on fuel, registering EPA economy ratings of 19 (city)/28 (highway) for the six-speed manual version.

arms and transmission mount were also upgraded. A Torsen Torque Sensing Limited Slip differential was available for an additional $999. This rear axle offered enhanced traction capabilities. Along with the Torsen rear axle came a Performance Lubricants package that included premium synthetic lubricants for the engine, power steering, and rear axle. This package was available separately for an additional $79. To help reduce engine-operating temperatures, an oil cooler was also available for $299. To top it all off, a special SS car cover and floor mats were available.

Chevrolet partnered with SLP (Street Legal Performance) to produce the 1996 SS-optioned Camaros. SLP had been involved with the modification of Pontiac's 1992 Firebird Firehawk. The excellent relationship that was built during that program encouraged Chevrolet to contract the work on the Camaro SS to SLP.

The basic Z28 was assembled at General Motors' assembly plant in Ste. Therese, Quebec, Canada. From there, those destined to become SS models were shipped to SLP's Montreal facility. Following alteration, the cars were shipped back to Ste. Therese for shipment to Chevrolet dealers. When a Camaro SS was purchased from a dealer, all of the

SLP modifications were covered by SLP's three year/36,000 mile warranty, while the balance of the vehicle was covered by GM's standard warranty. Chevrolet sold 2,410 1996 Camaro SS models in 1996.

In 1997, SLP upped the performance ante by producing a limited run of Camaro SS models powered by the 330-horsepower Corvette LT4 engine. For this special run of SS models, SLP performed engine swaps at its Montreal plant. The LT4 engines that were installed were hand-built and featured a new cam with a more aggressive profile, low-restriction exhaust, and a revised electronic control unit. Only 100 of these specially prepared SS Camaros were built for the American market.

When the 1998 Camaros were introduced, the Z28s and the SS-optioned Z28s were powered by the new 5.7-liter LS1 engine. The only thing the new engine has in common with the 350 that powered the original 1967 SS Camaro is the displacement. This all-new engine features the latest in materials, electronics, and engine design philosophy. The only thing the new LS1 lacks is the striking muscular appearance of the early big block engines.

The Camaro's LS1 is a tamed-down descendent of the 345-horsepower Corvette LS1. It features a deep skirt aluminum block that extends down past the main bearing caps. This allows the caps to be bolted vertically and horizontally, adding strength and durability. The heads are also cast aluminum and feature traditional two valves per cylinder with rocker arms and pushrods. Compression ratio is 10:1, the highest of any production car. A composite intake manifold is used for the sequential fuel injection, which provides the dual benefit of optimized fuel economy and performance. Under each Camaro LS1 is a cast aluminum oil pan that includes a sensor to detect when the engine is one quart low on oil. Attached to each long-life platinum tipped spark plug is its own ignition coil. The platinum plugs provide long life and the individual coils provide exceptional spark. The LS1 can easily purr along, taching 1,500 rpm at 70 miles per hour. Or when pushed, burning up the quarter mile in 13.7 seconds at 104 miles per hour, like SLP's Jim Mattison did for a *Muscle Car Review* Camaro SS road test in the November 1998 issue.

Other than adding a few new colors, Chevrolet didn't change a thing for the 1999 Camaro SS. The 2000 SS Camaros are powered by a stouter version of the LS1, rated at 320 horsepower. This new engine once again gives the SS package a performance edge over the standard Z28's 305-horsepower engine. Also added to the 2000 Camaro SS models are new wheels.

The Chevy Camaro has been a performance leader since it was introduced in 1967. Throughout the years, it has steadfastly maintained a performance image, even when it wasn't politically correct. Every time the Camaro's performance reputation has been challenged by a competitor, Chevrolet responds in spades and one-ups the competition.

Fill 'er Up–Ethyl

One thing almost all Super Sport models had in common from 1961 to 1970 was the requirement of premium fuel. An engine's compression ratio is the determining factor for the fuel required. Raising the compression ratio was an easy way of extracting more horsepower and most of the Super Sport engines had compression ratios of from 10:1 up to 11:1. In the 1960s, premium fuel was also known as ethyl. "Fill' er up–Ethyl," was a common phrase heard at a gas station when the attendant came to the driver's window of a Super Sport Chevy.

Few people realize that the advancements in gasoline technology were a direct result of two General Motors engineers, Thomas Midgely and Charles F. Kettering. Kettering, one of the great automotive innovators, had invented the electric self-starter and the battery-powered ignition for the 1912 Cadillac. Critics of the new electrical system blamed it for the engine's knock under certain conditions. Kettering felt that the engine's problem was not with the electronics, but with the fuel. He directed Midgely in an intensive research program.

On December 9, 1921, a spoonful of tetraethyl lead (TEL) was poured into the gas tank of a test engine that was set up to knock. Instantly the knocking stopped. Further testing proved that as little as one part of TEL to 4,000 parts of gasoline was effective in preventing knock. It took more than a year of experimentation to perfect the right combination with other elements to form the octane-boosting Ethyl fluid.

At that time, Standard Oil Company had been developing methods for producing TEL in large quantities. In 1924, Standard Oil and General Motors formed the Ethyl Corporation. Soon Ethyl was firmly established and its trademark became familiar to motorists across the country and around the world. The Ethyl Corporation continued research and eventually developed more than 50 other chemical products. In November 1962, General Motors and Standard Oil sold their interests in Ethyl Corporation to Albemarle Paper Manufacturing Company of Richmond, Virginia. In the early 1970s, due to the fact it contained a carcinogen, the TEL content in automotive gasoline was lowered and eventually removed completely.

The discovery of TEL as an antiknock compound and its development into a commercial product came about through long and painstaking research. TEL allowed higher compression ratios, which improved automobile performance and reduced fuel consumption. The development of TEL by General Motors engineers represented a substantial contribution to the internal combustion engine's ability to produce power.

The 1970 Chevy Monte Carlo was conceived as a low-cost personal luxury car. It was artfully crafted from a few Chevelle components. Chevy designers then worked within their cost constraints to create a stunning classic design.

Chapter 6

Monte Carlo SS

An Alchemy of Luxury and Performance

Throughout the 1950s and 1960s, Chevy and Ford battled for supremacy in the automobile market. One company would introduce a new car line and the other would counter with its own version. An excellent example was the 1953 Corvette, countered by the 1955 Thunderbird. Following that, it was Corvair versus Falcon and Camaro versus Mustang. One move that Chevrolet never responded to was the 1958 Thunderbird. That year, Ford enlarged the T-Bird to a four-passenger personal luxury car—effectively leaving the sports car class to Chevrolet's Corvette. Chevy and General Motors didn't attempt to match the larger T-Bird until 1963, when Buick brought out the beautifully styled Rivera. Then, in 1966, Olds introduced its Toronado, and in 1969, Pontiac released its Grand Prix.

Chevrolet management was concerned about not having a top-of-the-line personal luxury car. At the time, the best they had to offer was the Caprice. "The Caprice fit the old folks needs," says Dave Holls, Chevy's chief designer at the time. "We wanted something more youth-oriented than that." When Pete Estes took over as general manager of Chevrolet, he expressed an interest in this type of car. While he was at Pontiac, the Grand Prix had been developed. "We brought the proposals [for the Monte Carlo] out, and he bought it, hook, line and sinker," exclaims Holls. They started to work on a design, and a cost analysis was completed. "The Monte Carlo was amazingly reasonable, costing no more than $350 more than a Chevelle," chirps Holls. "That was a pretty elegant piece of machinery for only $350 more." At that time, money was important. Too much money into the project and it would have escalated the Monte Carlo into a higher price class, where it would have competed dollar for dollar with the Pontiac Grand Prix.

The traditional long-hood/short-deck, front engine car was the Monte Carlo's heritage. "What led the design a little were the regal proportions of the 1967 Cadillac El Dorado," recalls Holls. "Terry Henline did the whole project. He was a very bright young designer. There were a lot of good designs, but I picked his because I thought it was the best one of all." As the chief designer in the Chevrolet Studio, Holls' method was to let the designer who started the design follow it up. Henline continued with his design, knowing that the body wasn't going to be shared with any other car line. This gave him the freedom to create a car without input from other divisions. One of the many distinctive Monte Carlo features was that of two large headlights, instead of quad lights. General Motors' top-of-the-line models were to have quad headlights, and one proposal had them stacked vertically. The single pair of headlights and vertical taillights were designed to differentiate the Monte Carlo from the Chevelle. "We had to have something different [in the rear], because we were sharing the same deck with the Chevelle," says Holls. "We had to do something very dramatic. And those rear fenders were hard to make. We had to do a lot of adjustment to get that to stamp OK." Studio models are typically done in bright colors, but Holls wanted to play up the elegance of the new Monte Carlo. For the studio's fiberglass prototype model, he selected the gunmetal gray color and added the skirts.

"We never had anything thrown out; everybody liked that design," recalls Holls. Bill Mitchell, vice president of General Motors styling, and Pete Estes got along well and they both approved the design from full-size drawings before a clay model was ever built. "The only person who didn't like the Monte Carlo was Lee Mays, Chevrolet's sales manager. He just thought it was another car—he didn't know or like cars. Chevrolet had a lot of cars that year and he didn't know how to sell them. When he got the Monte Carlo, he didn't know what to do with it. He would have thrown away the biggest money maker! By '72, that car was making us a ton of money. What made that car so nice was that it was incredibly clean—and it cost us less than $350 per car to make it."

The 1970 Monte Carlo and the Pontiac Grand Prix were designated G-bodies, and like the Grand Prix, a majority of the Monte Carlo's components had A-body origins. The Monte Carlo was only available as a two-door coupe and its styling was aggressive, dramatic, and most of all, formal. It was also the most reasonably priced of all the personal luxury car offerings.

One of the most prominent features on the Monte Carlo was its stretched hood. To obtain the look designer Henline wanted, they had to elongate the A-body's 112-inch wheelbase to 116 inches. A new frame was designed that allowed for the extended front end. The overall length of the Monte Carlo was 205.8 inches, 8.6 inches longer than its A-body parent. Four inches were added in front of the cowl and an additional four inches were added to the front overhang. The front and rear tread on the Monte Carlo was nearly identical to the A-body 1970 Chevelle.

Viewed from the front, the Monte Carlo's grille was rectangular in shape. Inside the chrome frame were two thin horizontal bars backed by a tight egg-crate mesh, and mounted in the center was the new Monte Carlo crest. From above, the grille, bumper, and hood all blended into a slight V shape. On the center of the front of the hood was a small chrome spear. Two large round headlights dominated

The Monte Carlo's distinctive vertical taillights were one of the most difficult parts of the design to work out for production. The bright exhaust tips extending out from under the rear bumper were an exclusive part of the SS454 option.

The design theme of a long hood and short deck was very popular when the 1970 Monte Carlo was released. A minimal amount of chrome on the body accentuates the finely crafted sheet metal. The wide C-pillar, with its vertical leading edge, is one of the many design cues that indicate that this is an upscale car.

the front, and just below, in the bumper, were the circular parking lights. The front fenders and quarter panels were aggressively shaped, like those of the 1970 Chevelle, so instead of smoothly rounded blisters around the wheel openings, the flared area was more geometric and sharply defined without wheel lips. The Monte Carlo's wide C-pillar, with its vertical leading edge and small rectangular quarter window, was distinctively formal. Another formal touch was the addition of vertical taillights. The only bright trim on the body, other than around the

The deck lid of the 1970 Monte Carlo is a direct carryover from the 1970 Chevelle. To differentiate the rear from the Chevelle, Chevy designer Terry Henline placed the taillights vertically, giving a touch of elegance to the rear.

windows, was a thin molding that ran along the lower edge of the body. Integrated into this molding were the front and rear side marker lights. Thin bright moldings also outlined the wheel openings. In keeping with the overall clean design theme, Chevrolet imbedded the radio antenna into the windshield.

Fifteen solid acrylic lacquer colors were available on the 1970 Monte Carlo, along with seven two-tone combinations. Special wheel covers could be ordered, which included a body-color accent on the face of the cover. Vinyl tops were available in black, white, dark blue, dark gold, or dark green. Several materials were used on the standard bench seat interior, including a custom knit nylon and vinyl in black, blue, or green, and a pattern cloth and vinyl combination in blue, gold, or sandalwood. Strato bucket seats could be ordered in the custom knit nylon

and vinyl in black only or all vinyl in black, saddle, or dark green. The instrument panel was the same one that was fitted to the 1970 SS Chevelle, except the accents were in burled walnut.

The standard engine for the 1970 Monte Carlo was the 250-horsepower 350-ci small block. It was backed by a three-speed manual transmission. This was the only engine offered with the three-speed transmission. Optional were a four-speed manual, Powerglide, or Turbo Hydra-Matic. Optional engines included a 300-horsepower 350, a 265-horsepower 400-ci small block, or a 330-horsepower 402-ci big block, which was listed as a 400.

At the top of the engine list was the 360-horsepower 454. This engine was only available with the SS454 package. It featured oval-port cylinder heads with 10.25:1 compression, a hydraulic camshaft, and a cast-iron intake manifold with a Rochester

Quadrajet carburetor. The only transmission available for the SS454 was the Turbo Hydra-Matic 400.

The SS454 also included dual exhaust with special bright tips, a heavy-duty chassis (which included heavy-duty shocks, springs, and a rear stabilizer bar), 15x7-inch wheels and G70 white stripe tires. Standard as part of the SS454 option on the Monte Carlo was Automatic Level Control, which included Superlift rear shock absorbers that controlled the ride height by means of an engine-operated vacuum pump that supplied air when the rear suspension sensing valve indicated a change in ride height. The only exterior identification for the SS454 package was a small emblem on the lower body molding on the front fender. The emblem was very discreet—just the kind of thing a young street racer in a Mustang Mach I might overlook at a stoplight.

Motor Trend magazine road tested a 1970 Monte Carlo SS454, along with a 1970 Thunderbird and a 1970 Grand Prix. The Pontiac was powered with a 455-ci, 370-horsepower engine, and the T-Bird had a 360-horsepower 429 under the hood. The Monte Carlo bested the other two in performance by running 0–60 in 7.0 seconds and the quarter mile in 14.9 seconds at 92 miles per hour. *Motor Trend*'s writer Bill Sanders said, "The new Monte Carlo is an unqualified success in every respect."

The 1970 Monte Carlo SS454 was the type of car that could cruise Woodward Avenue on a Friday night begging for a stoplight skirmish, yet was also elegant enough to drive to a posh restaurant or opera house on a Saturday night. For many buyers in 1970, the new Monte Carlo filled the bill for a performance/family car that didn't intimidate many insurance companies.

In 1971, Chevrolet gave the Monte Carlo a light facelift, changing the pattern in the grille, revising headlight bezels, and utilizing rectangular parking lights. The SS454 option was again available, but now a four-speed manual could be specified, and the 15x7-inch Rally Wheels that had been optional in 1970 were included. In 1971, General Motors dropped the compression ratio on all its engines, including the Monte Carlo's 454, which fell to 8.5:1, yet horsepower jumped by 5 to 365. In the showroom, sales of the 1971 SS454 Monte Carlo faltered, with fewer than 2,000 sold, and in 1972 the SS454 package was dropped, along with anything that resembled a performance option. Two completely new versions of the Monte Carlo would come and go before there would be another SS option.

In the early 1980s, NASCAR racing began drawing a lot of attention, due in part to the expo-

The only exterior designation for the Super Sport option was the discreet placement of SS454 letters on the lower edge of the fender. The 15x7-inch wheels with G70 wide oval white stripe tires were standard. Rally wheels were optional; these have been chrome plated. The original ones were painted silver and fitted with trim rings.

sure it was receiving from cable TV and some smart marketing by the promoters. Names like Bill Elliot and Dale Earnhart were becoming more familiar and the Thunderbirds and Monte Carlos they drove at speeds of 200 miles per hour had a great deal of appeal. After a decade of cars that performed dismally, the cars of the 1980s were a breath of fresh air.

In 1983, Chevrolet had the daunting task of competing on the high-banks against the sleekly

The heart of the SS454 Monte Carlo was the 360-horsepower engine. Ordering the optional SS package was the only way a customer could get a 454 engine in a Monte Carlo. In 1970, the only transmission available with the 454 was the Turbo Hydra-Matic. The gold-colored cylinder on the right is the pump for the Automatic Level Control. Because of the extra-long front overhang, the Monte Carlo's engine compartment was enormous.

The Monte Carlo SS and the 1970 Chevelle SS shared the same instrument panel. On the Monte Carlo, the instrument panel's inlay was in wood-grain, keeping with its upscale image. The three large circular gauges from left to right are 7,000-rpm tach, 120-mile-per-hour speedometer, and clock. Bucket seats were not a standard part of the SS454 option, but they could be specified.

restyled Thunderbird. The new T-Bird was smoothly rounded, to which its low drag coefficient would testify. Chevrolet engineers sent the Monte Carlo into the wind tunnel for some testing, and the results showed that a new nose would help immensely, especially a flat face to reduce front end lift at speed. But for NASCAR to allow the revised Monte Carlo to compete on the track, Chevrolet had to make cars with the new nose available to the general public. Chevrolet put together a package on the Monte Carlo that included the new nose and a small deck lid spoiler. All the exterior bright trim was either removed or blacked out, special body stripes were added, and 15x7-inch Rally Wheels with P215/65R-15 Goodyear tires were included. All the assertive-looking package needed was a name, and with a simple stroke of genius and a few appropriately placed decals, the 1983 Monte Carlo was made into an SS.

After an 11-year absence, the Super Sport nameplate was reintroduced on the Monte Carlo in 1983. This 1985 model features the new front end developed for NASCAR. Blacked-out trim, body stripes, a small deck lid spoiler, and Rally Wheels with performance tires highlighted the Monte Carlo's exterior appointments. *Copyright 1978–1999 GM Corp. Used with permission of GM Media Archives*

Vince Piggins, Chevrolet's product promotion engineering manager, was the father of the Z28 and well known to anyone who raced a Chevy. He advocated changes to the new Monte Carlo SS that were more than stripes and fat tires. Specifically, Piggins believed the Monte SS should have an engine that matched its appearance, so the standard 305-ci small block was reworked to produce 175 horsepower. At the heart of the L69 engine was a Corvette camshaft and Rochester four-barrel carburetor, and the only available transmission was a Turbo Hydra-Matic. Underneath, there was a large-capacity, single Corvette catalytic converter, after which the 2-1/4 inch exhaust system branched into twin outlets. Also included with the 1983 Monte Carlo SS was a heavy-duty suspension and fast-ratio power steering.

All the 1983 Monte Carlo SS models were painted either white or dark metallic blue with con-

trasting stripes. The only interior available was a blue-and-white cloth and vinyl. Each of the headrests was stitched with a prominent SS logo and the instrument panel was fitted with the Monte Carlo's optional gauge package, which included a tachometer.

To proudly proclaim that Chevrolet was back in the musclecar business, 70 of the new 1983 Monte Carlo SSs were promenaded around the Daytona track prior to the running of the annual 500 mile race. These cars were then distributed to southeastern Chevy dealers to drive home to their showrooms. Chevrolet did everything right with the introduction and packaging of the 1983 Monte Carlo SS. These special models were well received, but because of the late introduction, only 4,714 SS-optioned Monte Carlos were built in 1983.

Because of the public's acceptance of the 1983 Monte Carlo SS package, Chevrolet offered it again in 1984. Externally, the 1984 model was unchanged,

In 1986, Chevrolet made a dramatic change to the Monte Carlo SS when it offered the Aero Coupe in limited numbers. The requirements of high-speed NASCAR racing required a new rear window that provided a fastback profile. The Monte Carlo SS with the Aero Coupe option was carried into 1988, when the Monte Carlo was discontinued and replaced by the new Lumina. *Copyright 1978–1999 GM Corp. Used with permission of GM Media Archives*

but under the hood, Chevrolet found five extra horsepower, boosting the total output to 180. Bucket seats were now an option and a new sportier steering wheel was added.

When *Hot Rod* magazine tested a new Monte Carlo SS in its March 1984 issue, writer John Baechtel couldn't type fast enough to get his enthusiastic impressions down on paper. This is how he opened his article. "The 1984 Monte Carlo SS gets our vote for 'Sleeper of the Year.' It satisfies all essential performance requirements and delivers them at a remarkably competitive price compared to contemporary performance cars. The Monte Carlo is just plain fun to drive, and with a reasonably healthy small block

Chevrolet introduced an all-new Monte Carlo in 2000. This car rode on the same platform used by the Pontiac Grand Prix, Buick Century, and Buick Regal. This increased the new Monte Carlo's wheelbase by 3 inches to 110.5 inches. This stretched wheelbase allowed Chevy's designers to develop a car with exciting proportions.

The 2000 Monte Carlo SS has four-wheel ABS disc brakes with 11.93-inch-diameter rotors in front and 11.0-inch rotors in the rear—the largest brakes of any midsize car. The SS rides on a special set of 16-inch-diameter, five-spoke wheels fitted with P225/60R-16 Goodyear Eagle RS-A performance tires.

under the hood, it gives that same good feeling you used to get from earlier intermediate performance cars like the 1966 Chevelle. While not as quick as some ancestors, with the F41 suspension option and 180 horsepower under the hood, the SS provides five-passenger comfort with stable handling and straight-line performance only a few tenths slower than the quickest cars available today." During *Hot Rod's* evaluation, the Monte Carlo SS ran the quarter mile in 15.39 seconds at 91.94 miles per hour. It also recorded admirable numbers on the skid pad. Baechtel wrapped up his article by saying, "The pricing and performance available in the Monte Carlo SS make it one of the most attractive buys for 1984." It had been a long time since automotive journalists had had an opportunity to say those kinds of things about anything produced in Detroit. Long

lines at the Chevy showrooms proved him right. Chevrolet sold 24,050 Monte Carlo SS models in 1984, which was roughly 18 percent of Monte Carlo production that year.

The momentum that the Monte Carlo SS developed in 1983 and 1984 continued into 1985. New for 1985 was a wider selection of colors, including black, dark maroon metallic, and silver metallic. White was still available as an exterior color, but the dark blue was dropped. New stripes in contrasting colors were used to highlight the SS package, and the interior colors were now maroon and gray with either buckets or bench seats. The only mechanical change to the 1985 model was the addition of the new 200-4R overdrive automatic as the standard transmission. T-tops were also added as an option in 1985. Sales were even stronger than the year

Thirty years of technological advancements have allowed the 200-horsepower V-6 in the new Monte Carlo to produce straight-line performance levels close to the original SS454 model. Cornering, braking, mileage, and overall driveability have improved immensely.

before, with the SS-optioned Monte Carlos totaling 30 percent of Monte Carlo sales.

At the outset of 1986, the only thing new on the Monte Carlo SS was the split bench seat option and aluminum wheels, but by midyear there came a dramatic change. The Monte Carlo's notch back roof had proven to be a detriment to NASCAR racers, so to remedy that, Chevrolet introduced the Monte Carlo SS Aero Coupe in limited numbers. A new special rear window was fitted to the Monte Carlo that provided a fastback profile. The fitting of this window required a severe shortening of the deck lid. The Aero Coupe option was carried into 1987 and early 1988, when the Monte Carlo was discontinued, at which time the Monte Carlo nameplate was shelved in favor of "Lumina."

The name *Lumina* never struck a chord with automotive enthusiasts. Monte Carlo evoked visions of wealth, Grand Prix racing, and royalty. Lumina

sounds like a new brand of bug light. In 1995, Chevrolet resurrected the Monte Carlo nameplate and added it to a restyled Lumina two-door. It was a good looking car and offered many of the elements that made the early Monte Carlo a success. A Z-34 performance option was available that offered some performance upgrades.

Chevrolet waited until the 2000 model year to play its SS trump card in a completely restyled Monte Carlo. Once again, aerodynamics and the demands of NASCAR racing drove the design program. On May 30, 1999, Chevrolet had two 2000 Monte Carlos ready in pace car trim for an auspicious introduction—one led the field at the Indy 500 and the other brought the thundering NASCAR Winston Cup cars to the green flag at the Coca-Cola 600.

The look of the 2000 Monte Carlo SS evokes the classic heritage of the original 1970 model with

The 2000 Monte Carlo SS is powered by Chevrolet's 3800 Series II V-6 engine. It features Sequential Fuel Injection (SFI) and a glass-reinforced composite intake manifold. Chevy's On-Board Diagnostics Second Generation (OBDII) is combined with the Powertrain Control Module (PCM) to control fuel delivery, ignition timing, and emissions systems. The only transmission available is the electronically controlled 4T65-E four-speed automatic overdrive. Traction control is standard on the SS Monte Carlo.

its long hood, short deck, and distinctive C-pillars. Even the taillights have the same vertical orientation as the 1970 model. But that's where the similarities end. Thirty years of technology have allowed the Monte Carlo to evolve into a car that is much safer, more fuel efficient, and more refined than the original version.

For the year 2000, the Monte Carlo's front tread was increased from 59.5 inches to 62.1 and the rear from 59.0 inches to 62.2. While the chassis dimensions grew, the overall length of the car shrank from 200.7 inches to 197.9—a feat that was accomplished with only small variances in interior and cargo space. In fact, most of the interior dimensions increased.

All Monte Carlos come with four-wheel ABS disc brakes. The Super Sport has 11.93-inch-diameter rotors in front and 11.0-inch rotors in the rear, giving the SS Monte Carlo the biggest brakes of any midsize car. The SS rides on a special set of 16-inch-diameter five-spoke wheels that are fitted with a set of P225/60R-16 Goodyear Eagle RS-A performance tires. MacPherson struts with special valving are used on all four corners, along with increased spring rates on the SS. To control body roll, there are 30-millimeter front and 17.2-millimeter rear stabilizer bars. Chevy's goal was to provide a ride that is predictable, comfortable, and responsive.

Under the hood, the 2000 Monte Carlo SS uses Chevrolet's 3800 Series II V-6 engine—the same 200-horsepower engine that powers the 2000 Im-

pala. The engine features sequential fuel injection and a glass reinforced composite intake manifold. An On-Board Diagnostics Second Generation (OBDII) is combined with the Powertrain Control Module (PCM) to monitor fuel delivery, ignition timing, and the emissions system. The only transmission available is the electronically controlled 4T65-E four-speed automatic overdrive, which has electronic controls to prevent engine overrevving in lower gears, as well as to continuously monitor driving conditions and automatically adjust shift quality to best suit the situation. Traction control is yet another SS standard feature.

In addition, the 2000 Monte Carlo SS offers every creature comfort anyone could ever want, including standard power windows, cruise control, leather-wrapped steering wheel with radio controls, tilt wheel, air conditioning with separate driver and passenger controls, power door locks, and the ultimate requirement in a modern car—cup holders. Leather seats are optional, as are power seats, heated driver and passenger seats, and a CD player.

The Monte Carlo has always been one of those cars that appealed to a wide spectrum of buyers. The Monte Carlo's luxury and refinement appeal to a more mature buyer, while the young driver gets the performance options in a well turned-out boulevard cruiser. The 2000 SS Monte Carlo continues that tradition in fine style.

Bibliography

Magazine & Periodical Articles

" '84 Monte Carlo SS." *Hot Rod* (March 1984).

"360 HP For Chevy II." *Hot Rod* (March 1962).

"1962–1967 Chevrolet Chevy II: Plucking Falcon's Feathers." *Collectible Automobile* (June 1993).

"1965–66 Chevrolet: When Bigger Was Better." *Collectible Automobile* (December 1993).

"1967–69 Camaro: Considered Response." *Collectible Automobile* (October 1990).

"1994 Chevrolet Impala SS." *Motor Trend* (June 1994).

"A Preretirement Chat With Chuck Jordan." *Collectible Automobile* (December 1992).

"Camaro: New Kid on the Block." *Hot Rod* (January 1967).

"Car Life Engineering Excellence Award." *Car Life* (February 1962).

"Chevelle 396." *Car Life* (September 1965).

"Chevrolet Impala Super Sport 409 V-8 with Powerglide." *Car Life* (March 1963).

"Chevrolet's Mystery 427 V-8." *Hot Rod* (May 1963).

"Chevy II 327/350 V-8." *Car Life* (May 1966).

"Chevy II Nova 327 Road Test." *Motor Trend* (July 1966).

"Chevy II Nova SS Road Test." *Car and Driver* (August 1968).

"Chevy II V-8 Road Test." *Motor Trend* (June 1964).

"Chevy II with a V-8." *Motor Trend* (March 1962).

"Chevy II." *Car Life* (February 1962).

"Chevy's New Flying Wedge." *Hot Rod* (March 1965).

"Chevy's Secret Weapon: The Nova SS." *Road Test* (May 1969).

"Earth Mover." *Hot Rod* (February 1970).

"Engineering the Chevy II." *Car Life* (February 1962).

"Living with Late Greats." *Late Great Chevys* magazine (June 1991).

"Martyr." *Special Interest Autos* (May-June 1974).

"Motor Trends." *Motor Trend* (June 1961).

"Power Beyond Belief." *Chevy Classics and Muscle Machines* (May 1999).

"Special: Super Sport Report." *Musclecar Classics* (June 1987).

"Spotlight On Detroit-'67 Cars." *Motor Trend* (July 1966).

"Spotlight on Detroit." *Motor Trend* (December 1962).

"Super Street Chevelle." *Hot Rod* (February 1966).

"Tech Analysis of the '68s - Chevy." *Hot Rod* (October 1967).

"The 1955 Chevrolet Reinvented: 1964–67 Chevelle." *Collectible Automobile* (August 1992).

"The Big Go West." *Hot Rod* (May 1961).

"Tres Chevelles." *Motor Trend* (July 1967).

GM Annual Report 1962, General Motors Corporation

GM Annual Report 1963, General Motors Corporation

GM Annual Report 1964, General Motors Corporation

GM Annual Report 1965, General Motors Corporation

GM Annual Report 1966, General Motors Corporation

GM Annual Report 1967, General Motors Corporation

GM Annual Report 1968, General Motors Corporation

GM Annual Report 1969, General Motors Corporation

Books

Bayley, Stephen. *Harley Earl and the Dream Machine.* New York, NY: Alfred A. Knopf Inc., 1983.

Boyce, Terry. *Chevy Super Sports,1961–1976.* Osceola, WI: MBI Publishing Company, 1981.

Colvin, Alan. *Chevrolet by the Numbers 1960–64.* Cambridge, MA: Robert Bentley Inc., 1996.

Colvin, Alan. *Chevrolet by the Numbers 1965–69.* Cambridge, MA: Robert Bentley Inc., 1994.

Cummings, David and Doris. *Chevrolet Book of Numbers Volume 2 1953–1964*, Blairsville, PA: Crank'en Hope Publications, 1989.

Editors of Consumer Guide. *Cars of the 60s.* Skokie, IL: Publications International, 1979.

Gunnell, John. *Illustrated Chevrolet Buyers Guide.* Osceola, WI: MBI Publishing Company, 1989.

Herd, Paul. *Chevelle SS Restoration Guide.* Osceola, WI: MBI Publishing Company, 1992.

Herd, Paul. *Chevrolet Parts Interchange Guide.* Osceola, WI: MBI Publishing Company, 1995.

Hooper, John. *Big Book of Camaro Data 1967–1973.* Osceola, WI: MBI Publishing Company, 1995.

Kimes, Beverly Rae and Robert C. Ackerson. *Chevrolet, a History From 1911–1986.* Kutztown, PA: Automobile Quarterly Publications, 1986.

Statham, Steve. *Camaro.* Osceola, WI: MBI Publishing Company, 1998.

Statham, Steve. *Nova SS.* Osceola, WI: MBI Publishing Company, 1997.

Wright, J. Patrick. *On a Clear Day You Can See General Motors.* Grosse Pointe, MI: Wright Enterprises, 1979.

Index